THIS BOOK IS DUE FOR RETURN ON OR
BEFORE THE LAST DATE STAMPED BELOW

000133	LESS RAIN
000142	Marion Mayr
000151	Polly Morgan
000158	MEGAN OLINGER
000163	Mike Joyce / Stereotype
000170	Will Sweeney
000179	ZAK KYES
000184	Stephen Preston
000192	Maziar Raein

WITHDRAWN

D1324006

BIS Publishers
International publisher for creative professionals

www.bispublishers.nl

Graphic is distributed by:

Australia
Tower Books
Unit 2, 17 Rodborough Road
Frenchs Forest, NSW 2086
T +62 2 9975 5566
F +62 2 9975 5599
E towerbks@zipworld.com.au
www.foliograph.com.au

Belgium
Bookstores
Exhibitions International
Kol. Begaultlaan 17
B-3012 Leuven
T +32 16 296 900
F +32 16 284 540
E orders@exhibitionsinternational.be
www.exhibitionsinternational.be

Other
Imapress
Brugstraat 51
B-2300 Turnhout

China & Hong Kong
Foreign Press Distributors Ltd
Room 6, Ground Floor, Block B
Proficient Industrial Center
6 Wang Kwun Road
T +852 2756 8193
F +852 2799 8840

France
Critique Livre Distribution SAS
BP 93-94 rue Malmaison
93172 Bagnolet Cedex
T +33 1 4360 3910
F +33 1 4897 3706
E critique.livres@wanadoo.fr

Germany
Bookstores
Gingko Press GmbH
Hamburger Straße 180
D-22083 Hamburg
Germany
T +49 40 291 425
F +49 40 291 055
E gingkopress@t-online.de
www.gingkopress.com

Germany, Austria & Switzerland
Distribution / Auslieferung
GVA Gemeinsame Verlagsauslieferung
Göttingen
Anna-Vandenhoeck-Ring 36
37081 Göttingen
Germany
T +49 551 487 177
F +49 051 413 92
E krause@gva-verlage.de

Other
ISS Pressevertrieb GmbH
Carl-Zeiss-Straße 5
D-53340 Meckenheim
T +49 22 258801 122
F +49 22 258801 199
E publishing@ips-pressevertrieb.de
www.ips-pressevertrieb.de

Indonesia
Aksara
Jalan Kemang Raya 8b
Jakarta 12730
T +62 21 7199 288
F +62 21 7199 282
E info@aksara.com
www.aksara.com

Italy
Happy Books SRL
Via Grandi 159
41100 Modena
T +39 059 454 219
F +39 059 450 343
E happy@happybooks.it

Idea srl
Via Lago Trasimeno, 23/2 (ZI)
36015 Schio (VI)
T +39 455 576 574
F +39 445 577 764
E info@ideabooks.it
www.ideabooks.it

Red Edizioni Sas
Viale Prampolini 110
41100 Modena
T +39 59 212 792
F +39 59 4392 133
E info@redonline.it

Librimport Sas
Via Biondelli 9
20141 Milano
T +39 2 8950 1422
F +39 2 8950 2811
E librimport@libero.it

Japan
Shimada Yosho
T.Place, 5-5-25, Minami-Aoyama, Minato-ku
Tokyo, 107-0062
T +81 3 3407 3937
F +81 3 3407 0989
E sales@shimada.attnet.ne.jp

Korea
Beatboy Inc.
Kangnam-Ku Shinsa-Dong 666-11
Baegang Building 135-897
Seoul
T +82 2 3444 8367
F +82 2 541 8358
E yourbeatboy@hanmail.net

Malaysia
How & Why Sdn Bhd
101A, Jalan SS2/24
47300 Petaling Jaya
Selangor
T +60 3 7877 4800
F +60 3 7877 4600
E info@howwwhy.com
www.howwwhy.com

Mexico
Books VIP, S.A. de C.V.
Fray Servando, Edif. 761-C-4
Jardín Balbuena C.P. 15900
México, D.F.
T +52 55 5764 4968
F +52 55 5764 4968
E info@booksvip.com
www.booksvip.com

The Netherlands
Bookstores
Betapress BV
Burg. Krollaan 14
5126 PT Gilze
T +31 161 457 800
F +31 161 457 224

Other
BIS Publishers
Herengracht 370–372
1016 CH Amsterdam
T +31 20 524 7560
F +31 20 524 7557
E bis@bispublishers.nl
www.bispublishers.nl

Russia
Design Books
3 Maly Kislovsky Lane office 315
Moscow 103009
T +7 095 203 65 94
F +7 095 203 65 94

Scandinavia and Eastern Europe
Gingko Press GmbH
Hamburger Straße 180
D-22083 Hamburg
Germany
T +49 40 291 425
F +49 40 291 055
E gingkopress@t-online.de
www.gingkopress.com

Singapore
Basheer Graphic Books
Block 231, Bain Street
#04–19 Bras Basah Complex
180231 Singapore
T +65 336 0810
F +65 334 1950

Page One Pte Ltd
20 Kaki Bukit View
Kaki Bukit Techpark II
415956 Singapore
T +65 744 2088
F +65 744 2088
E pageone@singnet.com.sg

Spain
ACTAR
Roca i Batlle 2 i 4
08023 Barcelona
T +34 93 418 77 59
F +34 93 418 67 07
E info@actar-mail.com
www.actar.es

Taiwan
Long Sea International Book Co., Ltd.
1/F No. 204 Si Wei Rd
Taipei 106 Taiwan ROC
T +886 2 2702 6838
F +886 2 2706 6109
E thfang@ms16.hinet.net
www.longsea.co.tw

Turkey
Evrensel Grafikir Yayincilik
Gulbahar Mahl
Gayret SK No:11
80300-01 Mecidiyekoy / Istanbul
T +90 212 356 7276
F +90 212 356 7278
E evrensely@superonline.com

United Kingdom
Bookstores
Airlift Book Company
8 The Arena
Mollison Avenue
Enfield, Middlesex EN3 7NL
T +44 20 8804 0400
F +44 20 8804 0044
E info@airlift.co.uk
www.airlift.co.uk

Other
Comag Specialist
Tavistock Works
Tavistock Road
West Drayton, Middlesex UB7 7QX
T +44 1895 433 800
F +44 1895 433 801

USA / Canada
Lords News International
133 Jefferson Avenue
Jersey City, NJ 07306
T +1 201 798 2555
F +1 201 798 5335
E support@lordsnewsinternational.com

All other countries
BIS Publishers
Herengracht 370–372
1016 CH Amsterdam
T +31 20 524 7560
F +31 20 524 7557
E bis@bispublishers.nl
www.bispublishers.nl

Subscriptions to Graphic

To subscribe contact:
Bruil & van de Staaij
PO Box 75
7940 AB Meppel
The Netherlands
T +31 522 261 303
F +31 522 257 827
E info@bruil.info
www.bruil.info

Subscription rates
1-year rate (2 issues)
including VAT and airmail:

NL: EUR 40
Europe: EUR 45
Other: USD 61

Student subscriptions: 20% discount
(valid only with a copy of your student
registration form)

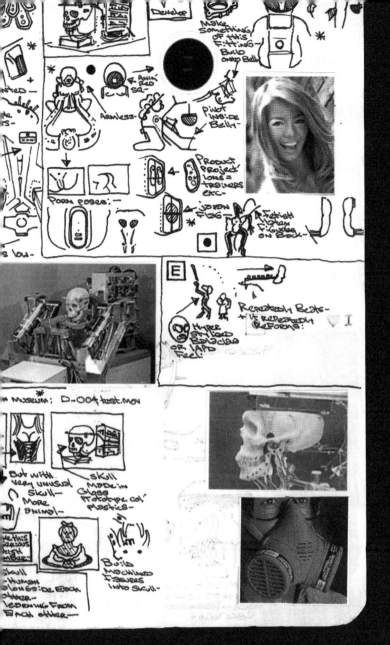

Graphic 10: Diaries
Graphic reveals everything!

Find out about
the most creative,
most explicit,
most graphic secrets!

In Issue 10, Graphic
gets really nosy
and naughty and
personal and asks
(well, kind of)
to peep into
the diaries and
the notebooks
in your drawers.

Email:
graphic@magmabooks.com

Sketchbooks courtesy of Johnny Hardstaff (pages 24–35)

P.S. If you don't keep
a diary – just lie,
invent, fake

Also forthcoming:
Graphic 11: Humour

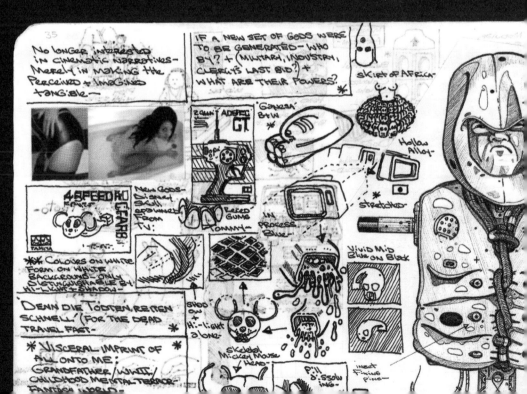

Benrik

**This Interview Will
Change Your Life –
The Twist In The Plot:
An interview with
Benrik**

by Marc Valli

**'Cult branding sounds
very pompous, which
we like.'**

I remember when I first came across **This Diary Will
Change Your Life***. It was piled up at the front of a
mainstream bookshop, alongside* **Harry Potter** *and*
*Julian Barnes and Jamie Oliver. I remember stopping,
frowning, picking one up, checking the publisher out
(in this case Penguin) and thinking, 'I just cannot
believe this…I just cannot believe these guys have
managed to pull this off!' The work of Benrik proves
that there is still space in that big, bad commercial
world out there, for someone to do their own thing in
their own way – and get away with it.*

YOUR
VALUES ARE
OUR TOILET
PAPER

*Marc: **Where do you come from?*** Benrik: Henrik is
from Sweden. Ben is originally from New Zealand,
although he grew up in France, and somehow managed
to end up speaking with a posh English accent. We
both now live in London. ***Marc: When did you meet?***
Benrik: We met in advertising five years ago. Henrik
had been working for TBWA Stockholm as an art
director, but moved to London in a hurry, for reasons
which he's never fully disclosed. Ben was a copywriter.
We teamed up and hit it off, as they say. Interestingly,
the very first copywriter Henrik teamed up with when
he got to London fled after three days, and hasn't been
heard of since. ***Marc: How did you get into business
together?*** Benrik: We kept coming up with ideas that
didn't fit into the traditional moulds of advertising. In
the end we realized they would never happen unless
we did them for ourselves. So we took the plunge, quit
our jobs, and started Benrik Limited. By far the most
time-consuming aspect was agreeing on the name. We
each think we fooled the other: Ben likes to think his
name is at the forefront of the company, and Henrik
claims that 5 out of the 6 letters are his. ***Marc: You
do a lot of self-initiated work; do you also work with
clients? If so, how do they react to your approach?***
Benrik: So far, we've mostly been doing our own
thing. *This Diary Will Change Your Life* is extremely
time-consuming, as we have to design each page in a
totally different style, and we do 99% of it ourselves,
from writing to illustration, typography, photography

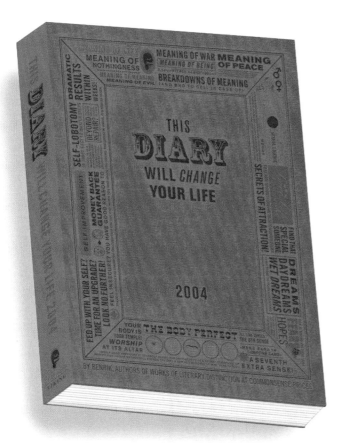

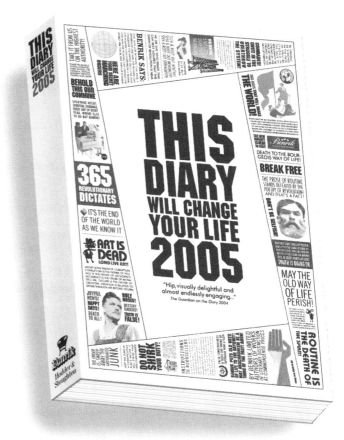

*This Diary Will Change
Your Life*
Covers of the *Diary* from
2004–2006.

etc. It is commercial work though, in the sense that it has to sell straight to consumers in a very competitive market. So we can't afford to be self-indulgent, and that approach translates well to real clients. We've done a couple of things, a stationery range for a PR company, and a book for ad agency Mother, with whom we share offices. This year we're looking to take on more clients, though it's important that we should all be on the same wavelength. We don't want to create communication that whacks people over the head with a huge media spend. We call what we want to do 'cult branding' – brand content that adds to the culture and that people actually want to buy into, like our *Diary*. 'Cult branding' sounds very pompous, which we like.

***Marc: Humour seems to be a very important part of
your style. Do people always get the joke?*** Benrik:
Yes and no. We like to leave some room for ambiguity, so that the reader has to work out if we're joking or not. And in fact, sometimes we are both joking and not joking. The Diary tasks are meant to be funny and surreal of course, but equally, if you follow them for real, your life will change, no question. Some tasks are obviously more deranged than others, like: 'Go dogging as a Jehovah's witness'. But some are very serious, like: 'Today, make sure your parents know you love them'. We've sold over 350,000 books worldwide now, and one thing we have noticed is that

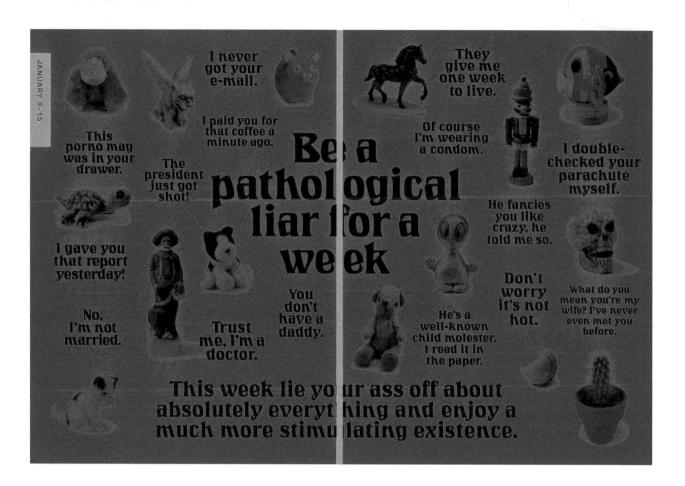

I never got your e-mail.

This porno mag was in your drawer.

I paid you for that coffee a minute ago.

The president just got shot!

They give me one week to live.

Of course I'm wearing a condom.

I double-checked your parachute myself.

Be a pathological liar for a week

I gave you that report yesterday!

No, I'm not married.

Trust me, I'm a doctor.

You don't have a daddy.

He fancies you like crazy, he told me so.

He's a well-known child molester. I read it in the paper.

Don't worry it's not hot.

What do you mean you're my wife? I've never even met you before.

This week lie your ass off about absolutely everything and enjoy a much more stimulating existence.

This Diary Will Change Your Life
Spreads from the *Diary*.

Above
Be a pathologial liar for a week

Opposite, above
This week, volunteer for a medical experiment

Opposite, below
This week, act like you're invisible

'In an ideal world, you would have a team of people to produce every idea as it floats out of your brain. If we were billionaires, that's what we would spend our money on'

Americans tend to treat the tasks more seriously. They follow them religiously. And that's great. In the UK, everyone is so cynical and ironic that everything gets treated as a joke. We'd much rather look at things with a naive innocence, like a particularly slow child. When we created the *Diary,* we didn't intend it to be perceived purely as a humour title; we wanted it to work on several levels. Big bookshop central computer systems prefer to pigeonhole you though; if you're not in one single category, staff just don't know where to put you. *Marc: Do you work around a story? A narrative?* Benrik: Our work so far has been, in a sense, a parody of self-help culture (we call it 'extreme self-help'). So, formally, like self-help advice, it tends to consist of little individual nuggets of wisdom, rather than a straightforward story or narrative. Taken together, though, they probably add up to a story, the story of someone who's confronted with what looks like an infinite number of choices, but who, strangely, craves direction – which we are happy to provide. *Marc: How do ideas emerge?* Benrik: Ideas are the easy and fun part. It's editing and polishing the best ones that takes time and effort. In an ideal world, you would have a team of people to produce every idea as it floats out of your brain. If we were billionaires, that's what we would spend our money on. We are mystified that the super-rich these days do nothing interesting or creative with their money, no pyramids, no Xanadus, nothing. We are thinking of contacting

them to make a few suggestions. *Marc: Do you do a lot of research?* Benrik: The *Diary* covers every aspect of life, so yes, we need to research stuff, though we don't hesitate to rewrite the facts to make them fit the Benrik mindset. We've written a *History of the Diary,* for instance, which is basically a history of the world reinterpreted knowing that the *Diary* has shaped it throughout. Lenin, for instance, started the Russian revolution after following a 1917 *Diary* dictate for example. This required a fair bit of historical twisting and turning. *Marc: Do things you see or read come into your work?* Benrik: Everything is grist to the Benrik mill. We are big news consumers, and find that anger at the world is a good source of creative inspiration. English philosopher Bertrand Russell said that as a leftward-leaning student, he had 'strong views, weakly held'. Having a point of view on things is crucial, even if you change it every now and again. It's important to get your knowledge and opinions from dramatically different sources. Probably because we're both from outside the UK, we find the British media very conformist and narrow-minded – the broadsheets as much as the tabloids. The worst is BBC local news: positively fascist. *Marc: Do you watch TV? What do you watch?* Benrik: There is no one secret channel or single source of alternative data. We are very eclectic in our readings and viewings. We find that distrusting most information is as useful a method as anything. We like channels and media that reveal a

This week, volunteer for a medical experiment

Drugs companies need to test their new products on human volunteers. You can earn decent cash by participating in their trials. But it's not about the money, it's about the unrivalled opportunity for radical life change. These are drugs in the early stages of development, before research has sanitized them. Pick a cutting-edge drug, and chances are you'll develop cutting-edge side effects: night vision, telepathy or radioactive superpowers perhaps. Think of how that would pep up your daily routine! Call today and volunteer your services.

Contact: most of the large pharmaceutical companies have clinical research divisions. Or visit www.thiswebsitewillchangeyourlife.com for details.

Worst-case scenario: you'll be able to bring an expensive lawsuit!

A strain of human DNA

Where do I sign up?

Not so fast! To qualify for most clinical trials, you should be a healthy male aged 18–45. Women aged 18–65 may apply but usually need to be post-menopausal or infertile, as the danger to any fetus from these trials is too great. However, if you are very keen, ask if you may sign a legal waiver. You will need to undergo a medical check-up to ascertain your suitability. You will usually be asked to stay overnight, and will be expected to attend daytime clinics for blood tests and other forms of monitoring. Important: Make sure to ask for early Phase I trials, or even volunteer for late-phase animal trials if you want to guarantee noticeably life-changing results. Our tip: invasive trials pay better.

Case studies

(these examples starting this week are fully-booked, but others like them are available)

Start date	Monday 11/12/06	Monday 11/12/06	Monday 11/12/06	Tuesday 12/12/06	Friday 15/12/06	Friday 15/12/06	Sunday 17/12/06
Study code	JS0098X	Sanuspol 3000z	Phfx/788/ fact.4	TT-x545	RD2100000 M7	DRF003/ 2a	Ch56/ 44-0004
Study type	New laxative drug	Kidney cleansing agent	Cancer vaccine	Drug side-effects on spinal fluid	Skin reaction to GM bio-enzyme YK9	Blood recoagulant	Potential vaccine for Marburg haemorrhagic fever
Country	UK	UK	Belgium	UK	USA	Andorra	Tasmania
Overnight stays	1	1	4	5	7	1 to 14+ (depending response)	59
Daily visits	Medical x2 morning visits	Medical	Medical x3, annual check-up (indef.)	Medical x2, annual check-up for 6 years	Medical x2, 12 monthly visits	Medical x3	Medical, 2 month stay
Risk factor	6/10	2/10	7/10	8/10	8/10	8/10	9/10
Payment	£1,450	£190 + travel expenses	£2,500	£4,125	$2,200	£1500 min	£6,980 + airfare

This week, act like you're invisible

Experience one of mankind's oldest moral quandaries: what would you do if you could get away with anything? Plato tells the tale of Gyges, shepherd to the King of Lydia, who finds a golden ring that confers invisibility on he who wears it. As soon as he realizes his power, Gyges goes to the court where he sleeps with the Queen and assassinates the King, taking his place. You may not want to go quite as far, but explore your hold on justice nonetheless. Would you steal, grope, murder? As ever, Benrik's legal disclaimer applies...

Collective task: on Thursday at 10am, everyone gather in the Assyrian section of the British Museum (Room 6) and strip naked of that a French tourist you see. When she guards turn up, collectively testify that none of you were even in the room at the time, and that she must have imagined the whole incident.

'As we deal in "extreme self-help", relationship books were obviously a rich area. We also like the idea of Benrik being the third party in people's relationships'

This spread
The Couple's Book
The indispensible companion to any self-respecting relationship

lot about their viewers' psyche, like the teleshopping ones. The English Al-Jazeera should be interesting, as long as they keep it anti-Western. And the God Channel makes for hours of fascinating viewing.

Marc: Where do you work from? What's the office or the studio like? Do you have many assistants running around the office making you coffee? Benrik: We work from the Biscuit Building in Shoreditch, in a huge open-plan office with lots of different typical Shoreditch companies, designers, website types, TV, etc. The only thing that separates us all are these plastic abattoir curtains. Nathan Barley would feel right at home. We do occasionally bring people in to help, both designers and work experience assistants. They don't make coffee, but they definitely get their hands dirty. We always have half a dozen projects on the go, from the books to TV ideas to 3G. Eventually, we'll end up employing people full-time. ***Marc: Who's the boss?*** Benrik: Benrik, of course. We're both very opinionated. The way it works is that we have to agree on things. If we don't, then we look for another solution until we're both happy. ***Marc: Does art pay – in the end?*** Benrik: Not as well as crime.

Marc: How did Love Life & Couple's Book ***come about?*** Benrik: Few areas are so full of clichés as relationships. It's the new religion of our time and,

paradoxically, the people most obsessed with them are least likely to make a success of it. And as we deal in 'extreme self-help', relationship books were obviously a rich area. We also liked the idea of Benrik being the third party in people's relationships. The book's subtitle is *The Indispensable Companion To Any Self-Respecting Relationship.* What interested us was creating the first book designed for two people. Books are normally a very private experience. Here, you are supposed to read it together, write in it together, hold it together. We even wanted to make it compulsory to buy it together, but bookshops vetoed that one.

Marc: Is a lot of it drawn from personal experience? Benrik: No, the point was to parody the universal rules which are supposed to govern all relationships. So the personal touch would have been out of place. Although, we do showcase our other halves in 'author's photos'. As we say, they are prettier than us, and we thought women flicking through would be more likely to buy it if they assumed it was written by two ladies…

Marc: What was the idea behind This Diary Will Change Your Life? Benrik: The idea was 'extreme self-improvement'. There are various inspirations – *The Dice Man*, the saying that 'you should do something that scares you everyday', the mindless culture of self-help. There is a huge hunger for change and excitement, yet the options on offer are limited.

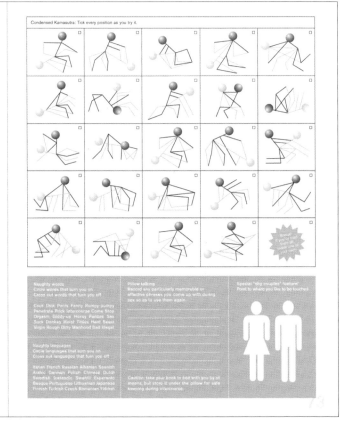

We think these limitations are largely mental. Even if you don't follow the tasks for real, the *Diary* expands your imaginary horizons. ***Marc: You seem to always be trying to engage the reader directly, do you get many reactions from readers or people who bought your products?*** Benrik: The *Diary* is a child of the internet. The web has brought people together in original ways, which has led to new real-life social patterns, like flashmobs for instance. Translating some of that virtual interactivity into a diary format has given it a connection with the real world. And we've seen that through our website. People register, over 3,500 write blogs everyday about following the tasks, they make friends, and eventually they meet up for real (in what they call 'Benrikmeets', organised totally independently of us). Our site is very active, although we don't subscribe to the traditional view of the internet, which is of an open access democracy. We run a tight ship, and occasionally purge users randomly. This keeps the others on their toes, and makes them feel special for having survived the cull. It's like a slightly sado-masochistic loyalty scheme.

Marc: The diaries all seem to have a theme, do you already have the theme of the next one? Benrik: They don't have a theme in the sense that the Redstone diaries do. But every time we try to push things further, involve people more. This year's theme emphasizes the cult aspect of Benrik. We are working

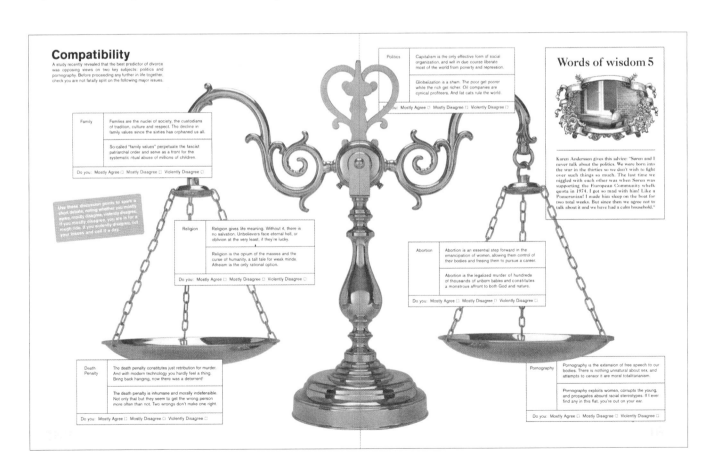

'Someone paid over £80 to have dinner with us. It was very awkward to begin with, but he was less of a nutter than he could have been'

Below
Buddhist Fundamentalism Week
The indispensible companion to any self-respecting relationship

Opposite
Don't Jump!
'Anti-suicide' promotional campaign for the 2006 Diary. The posters were affixed to the railings of major London bridges.

on having sleeper cells, sleeper readers who will awaken to promote our books at a predetermined date. *Marc: You have worked with a different publisher every time. Why?* Benrik: It hasn't been deliberate. We've had a run of bad luck with publishers. The first one fired our editor just before launch. The second one priced the *Diary* at £17.99, then acted surprised when it didn't sell as well. We're now with Macmillan, who are very good, although we're already onto our third editor there … Perhaps we're jinxed. *Marc: Did they ever censor any of your work?* Benrik: Overall, we've been remarkably free, certainly much more so than we were in advertising. And we try not to go for gratuitous shock, anyway; it's too easy. There have been a few half-hearted attempts at censorship. One of our editors had a strong aversion to the word 'masturbation'. Another had issues with references to drugs, even though the page in question was anti-drugs. Recently we've noticed a kind of corporate squeamishness about terrorism. There's a task in this year's *Diary* calling on people to become 'fundamentalist buddhists', motto: 'relax or we kill you!' They tried to argue Buddhists could take offence, which is ridiculous as the concept praises Buddhism for being the only sane religion; the idea of a gun-toting Buddhist is self-evidently preposterous. A lot of it is to do with the new anti-religious hatred legislation. The real harm won't come from actual prosecutions, but from corporate lawyers watering down material just to be on the safe side. Unsurprisingly, we are freedom of speech extremists. *Marc: Tell us a bit about the 'appear on a Benrik cover' competition. Was it serious? Did you really take the winner out for dinner?* Benrik: Anyone who publishes a book soon learns to dread book signings in bookstores, which constitute a novel form of degradation for all involved. In any case, we try to provide a new angle on any format we touch. So at Selfridges last year, instead of just signing books, we took polaroids of people with the promise that one of them, picked out at random, would be on our next cover and achieve their fifteen minutes of fame. Hundreds of wannabes had their photos taken, and a lovely woman named Margaret Elliott got her name and photo on the cover of the *Diary*. This year, a Swedish woman won it, so she'll be on next year's cover. The dinner story is separate. We had a task which was, 'Today, bid for dinner with Benrik at the Ivy on eBay!' When we wrote it ages ago, it seemed like an abstract joke, but as the date neared we realized we would have to deliver. So we booked a table at the Ivy, and put ourselves up on eBay. For a while, the only person who bid was our agent, but then there was a last-minute bidding war amongst our readers, and someone paid over £80 to have dinner with us. It was very awkward to begin with, but he was less of a nutter than he could have been, and we enjoyed ourselves a lot.

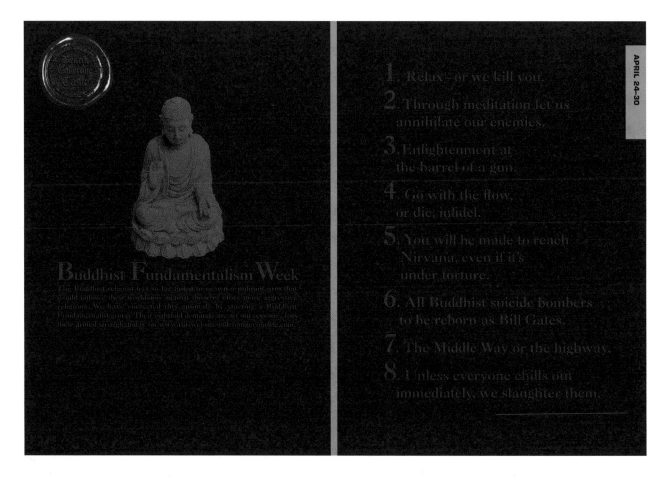

APRIL 24–30

1. Relax – or we kill you.
2. Through meditation let us annihilate our enemies.
3. Enlightenment at the barrel of a gun.
4. Go with the flow, or die, infidel.
5. You will be made to reach Nirvana, even if it's under torture.
6. All Buddhist suicide bombers to be reborn as Bill Gates.
7. The Middle Way or the highway.
8. Unless everyone chills out immediately, we slaughter them.

DON'T JUMP!

THIS **DIARY** WILL CHANGE **YOUR LIFE** 2006

OUT NOW

Fine Dine with Benrik tonight!

The highest bidder on ebay (search for: Benrik) gets to enjoy dinner with the authors of the Diary at London's exclusive Ivy restaurant tonight at 8pm.

What's included
If you bid £5-10: we go dutch
If you bid £10-20: the aperitifs are on us
If you bid £20-50: Benrik pay for the drink
If you bid £50-£100: we'll shout you dessert
If you bid £100-£500: the whole meal is on us
If you bid £500-£1000: we tell you the secret of our success
If you bid £1000 and upwards: one sexual favour of your choice

Wednesday 2 November

8		14	
9		15	
10		16	
11		17	
12		18	
13		19	

Marc: You mention the internet a couple of times. How do you see its future? Benrik: We are technologically illiterate, which in some ways is very useful. We think of ideas that the experts don't; we've been wanting to create a second, rival internet for years now, and have struggled to find a web professional who can even contemplate the concept. Possibly it's because it's ridiculous, possibly not. What we're interested in is the need for curating, particularly as self-generated content takes over. We don't believe in the current free-for-all. 'Benrik Internet' would feature thousands of employees filtering out the content we don't like, Chinese-style.
Marc: Who would you say are the people who most influenced you? What would your 'love hit parade' be like when it came to art & design? Benrik: We don't particularly study trends in design. We probably like people with a more conceptual approach, and an interesting voice, like David Shrigley or Banksy. In fact David Shrigley contributed a 'guest day' in the 2005 *Diary*: 'You must stop horsing around. Your life up until today has been nothing but horseplay and now it's time to stop it, you idiot'. But generally speaking, we're too busy doing our own stuff to follow other people's.

Marc: Do you read a lot? What do you read? Benrik: We only read our own books. It's a matter of principle. One thing most people don't realize is that writing a book ruins bookshops for you. You can't just go in and have a peaceful browse anymore. You seek out your book, and look at where it's placed. If you don't like where it's placed, you discreetly shift it to a better position. If it's not there at all, you go up to the counter and ask if they have it, anonymously, like that flyfishing chap in the old Yellow Pages ad. Staff snigger at you behind your back. It's pretty tragic.
Marc: What project(s) are you most involved with at the moment? Benrik: The book for Mother is taking some time, but will be beautiful. We hope to sell it to the public for £99.99. We are also working on the next *Diary*, out in October. We encourage *Graphic* readers to contribute ideas for tasks through our website – many of the concepts now come from our readers, which adds to the cult aspect. We hope that one day they will write the whole thing and we will lie on a beach somewhere. We also spend a lot of time on PR, not just because we're publicity-hungry, but because it's an artform in its own right. Last year we sent a video to Osama Bin Laden via Al-Jazeera, in which we explained the idea behind the *Diary* and suggested he should follow it to change his life in 2005. The chief editor of Al-Jazeera said he couldn't guarantee delivery, so we put it up online as well. This year, we created an anti-suicide campaign, with posters on all the major London bridges saying, 'Don't jump! *This Diary Will Change Your Life*, out now.' We also do more serious stuff. In 2004, we created www.globalvote2004.org with our friends at Poke; this was a site that allowed non-Americans to vote in the US presidential elections. It got over one million hits in a month, and was covered on CNN, Reuters, *New York Times*, Channel Five etc. Kerry won of course, which shows the limitations of the internet. We also got a lot of angry emails from Americans, calling us 'linguine-spined Europeans'. *Marc: What's your PR strategy?* Benrik: So far, it's been fairly scattergun. If we spot an opportunity to do something that tickles us, we do it – like the anti-suicide poster, or *globalvote*, we go ahead and do it. We advertised one *Diary* by having a fan eat it in Waterstones, Piccadilly (except for the hardback cover, of course). Our strategy is to sow lots of little PR seeds, and hope that a couple

إذ هو كثيراً كثيراً تحتاج طرقك في العالم بأن تتغير). Osama.

Opposite page
Fine Dine With Benrik Tonight
This *Diary* task instucts readers to bid on eBay for dinner with Benrik. The winner paid over £80.

Left
Video message for Osama
Sent via Al-Jazeera, the video encourages Osama Bin Laden to buy the 2005 *Diary* in order to change his life.

Below
Baby T-shirt
From the Benrik range, available at www.benrik.co.uk

will germinate. *Marc: What is your most ambitious / outrageous plan for the future?* Benrik: Eventually we want to become a kind of twisted Disney, a warped entertainment empire. We envisage Benrikland, a funpark where kids will shoot off into space, never to return – Hansel and Gretel on an industrial scale. Although we like kids, a lot of our fans are actually teachers, and some of them get their classes to follow the *Diary*. We also have a cool T-shirt range, available through the site. On the label we claim they're 'guaranteed handmade by a 12-year-old illegal immigrant named Pablito'. (Note that this is a joke, of course. In actual fact the truth is the opposite. And by that we don't mean that the illegal immigrant is called Juan…)

Marc: Let me now just ask you a few questions that relate to this issue in particular. How would you define your character? Benrik: Benrik is a Swedo-New Zealand-Frenchman, with a Russian wife, a child, and an English girlfriend. Slightly schizophrenic overall. *Marc: Who is your ideal audience?* Benrik: ABC1s with an 18–30 skew and poetico-anarchistic leanings. *Marc: What's your kryptonite?* Benrik: Cheap champagne. *Marc: Who are the good guys, who are the bad guys?* Benrik: We are the good guys, the axis of goodness. The bad guys are the terrorists, everyone knows that. *Marc: What's the happy ending?* Benrik: This is it!

* * *

This Diary Will Change Your Life 2006 is published by Boxtree, price £9.99

www.benrik.co.uk

'Eventually we want to become a kind of twisted Disney, a warped entertainment empire. We envisage Benrikland, a funpark where kids will shoot off into space, never to return'

Mori Chack

**Beating The Crap
Out Of Pity:
An interview
with Mori Chack**

by Richard Brereton

Mori Chack is the creator of many characters but is perhaps best known for the story of the boy Pity and his combative relationship with Gloomy bear.

Richard: Tell me about your childhood in Osaka.
Mori: It was on the quiet side. I used to doodle on everything. When I started school I filled textbooks, notebooks and desks with doodles. I didn't pay much attention in class. My grades were rock bottom, but on the bright side my artistic ability and imagination were developing nicely. *Richard: Violence is a recurrent theme in your work. Did you fight with your siblings?* Mori: Sure, my elder brother and I were very close in age. My mom always had to step in. I cried a lot.

Richard: When did you start drawing? Mori: Ever since I can remember. *Richard: What kind of things?* Mori: War heroes, animated robots. I probably watched a lot of that kind of thing on television. In second grade I drew a lot of cars, Porsche and BMW racing cars. They were pretty bad. *Richard: When did you create the bear character Gloomy?* Mori: In 2000, he was created while I was doodling at work. Some things never change. *Richard: Why was Gloomy abandoned by his parents?* Mori: No specific reason, probably the same reason dogs and cats are abandoned. The owners just can't keep them anymore. *Richard: Was it because he's pink?* Mori: That's a new angle. I guess when people choose a pet they do care about things like breed, colouring and size. Everyone wants a pet that they think is cute. But along those lines, I think it would be hard to abandon a pink pet. Unless you hate pink, that is. *Richard: Yeah, pink might not work for me. Where did Pity find Gloomy and is Pity based on you?* Mori: I haven't disclosed exactly where Gloomy was found, but in my mind it was in an empty lot, or on the side of the road, just like any other dog or cat. I've never personally picked up a bear, but I have picked up dogs and cats. So, my experience is definitely reflected in that sense. *Richard: Can you explain the nature of their violent relationship?* Mori: I had many pet cats when I was

'Everyone wants a pet that they think is cute. But along those lines, I think it would be hard to abandon a pink pet. Unless you hate pink, that is.'

This page, top right
Mori Chack

This page, right
1981
Mori's childhood sketchbook

Opposite page
Pity and Gloomy

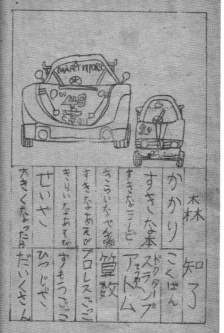

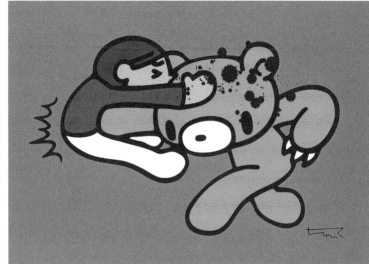

young. They bit and scratched me daily. If you think about it, it's just that cats are smaller and weaker than humans. If this were a lion or a bear, I would have been fatally wounded. But that same violent cat would turn right around and cuddle up to me and rub itself against me. Even if humans could explain such bizarre animal behaviour, it would simply be a limited guess and therefore meaningless. I mean, would you hate your pet just because it scratched you? *Richard: I guess not. Would you describe the relationship between Pity and Gloomy as unhealthy, co-dependent or a kind of love story? Where are they going?* Mori: Just like cats and dogs, Gloomy grows at a much faster rate than humans, so inevitably they will have to say farewell.

Richard: There's a new film by Werner Herzog called Grizzly Man *about a man who's killed by wild bears. Will Gloomy ever kill Pity?* Mori: No, other than dying of old age, which is inevitable. I do not want to kill any of my characters. If I can prevent that from happening, I certainly will. *Richard: If you had to choose, do you see their relationship becoming less violent or more loving?* Mori: I think more loving, in the sense that Pity continues to love Gloomy no matter how badly he is beaten up. It's not unlike a physically abusive relationship between a parent and child. *Richard: I see. Do Pity or Gloomy ever feel physically or mentally unwell?* Mori: You could say that Pity's unwillingness to abandon Gloomy no matter what he does to him is 'sick' in a way. But when you love anything so unconditionally, be it a person or even a hobby, it is unhealthy. You lose sight of everything around you. You become

'My cats bit and scratched me daily. If you think about it, it's just that cats are smaller and weaker than humans. If this were a lion or a bear, I would have been fatally wounded.'

unable to do anything else. I think everyone has experienced that before. ***Richard: Oh, I have. When I was a little boy I had a pet rabbit called Snowy. One day the neighbour's dog jumped the fence. The dog circled Snowy for a while, then bit off her head. Do you have any traumatic stories?*** Mori: I had a pet chick once, I let him loose in front of the house and a neighbour stepped on him accidentally. He died instantly of course, with all his guts squished out. What I remember most was my mom crying and burying him on the side of the house. I was about five years old. ***Richard: That was about the same age as me and Snowy. I understand the Gloomy toys have been very successful. How many Gloomy toys have been made so far?*** Mori: I've lost count. Several companies make them so it's hard to keep track. But it would be interesting to find out. ***Richard: How do people react to your toys?*** Mori: People have such different senses of values, so I can't generalize. But I can say that there is a hundred and eighty degree difference between the reactions of those who are on the same wavelength as me, and those who aren't. But to have opposing views is human nature and a healthy sign, I think. ***Richard: Do you ever get complaints from parents?*** Mori: No, they're ecstatic about it. ***Richard: Are the toys aimed more towards adults?*** Mori: No. Not at all. They're for everyone and anyone, regardless of age – whomever understands my work.

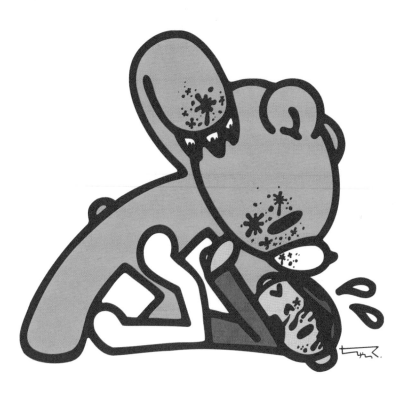

'I've upgraded my residence and my car. I also have the luxury of ordering salads when I dine out.'

Richard: What would you compare the toymaking process to? Mori: I haven't thought about it like that. I guess it would be like carrying on a conversation with a woman. You have to be entertaining, never boring. You have to listen carefully, be sensitive to trends, keep up the energy and avoid those silences. *Richard: Do you manage that?* Mori: I think I do… *Richard: Are you a toy collector?* Mori: I used to collect animated comic toys but I've given them away to friends since my place is overflowing with my own. *Richard: Has Gloomy made you rich? If so, how rich?* Mori: Well, I've upgraded my residence and my car. I also have the luxury of ordering salads when I dine out. And there's only 100% pure juice in my refrigerator now. *Richard: You have other characters, but it seems Gloomy is the most popular. Do you know why this is?* Mori: I wonder. I guess Gloomy just had 'something' that grabbed people's hearts. I'd like to hear from the fans what that 'something' is. *Richard: Do you sometimes get jealous of Gloomy's popularity?* Mori: No. Gloomy is simply a part of my mind that has been physically incarnated. In a way, Gloomy is me, so his popularity would never make me jealous. Only very, very happy.

Richard: Work-wise and personally, what's your next story? Mori: I would love to develop myself further overseas. If there's an opportunity to do a book signing that would be nice. *Richard: Mr Chack, thank you and please send my regards to Gloomy.*

* * *

www.chax.net

Johnny Hardstaff

Strange Places: An insight into the rich and complex into the mind of graphic artist and filmmaker Johnny Hardstaff – from working at a mortuary to hanging out in the Royal College of Surgeons and the Veterinary College or the V&A's National Library.

A profile of Johnny Hardstaff by Marc Valli

'The beauty of graphic design today is that its practitioners approach filmmaking and animation with a completely different set of sensibilities. We are all familiar with how directors approach cinema. We've seen it for a hundred-odd years.'

Got Any Glue?

Marc: Tell us a bit about your story? Johnny: I was brought up in the Midlands. The Midlands is the Hardstaff's traditional breeding ground. I often return there to mate. The Hardstaffs were once mercenary staff fighters in Nottinghamshire's forests. They would be paid to beat people. I sometimes wonder if working in the media is a modern day extension of this. In the early nineties I left the Midlands to study Graphic Design at St. Martins School of Art, and upon graduation, avoided all things design like the very plague. I felt rather uninspired by the decade and the options that were then open to me in design, so I opted to do absolutely anything else. I worked in a hospital mortuary. I delivered meat. I worked at New Covent Garden's fruit and vegetable market. I travelled around and lived abroad. All sorts of adventures. But I kept sketchbooks incessantly. I still do. Compulsively. I knew that I'd want to get involved in design again, but I wanted to do it my way, with my aesthetic and my principles. I didn't want to try and slot into someone else's 'movement'. ***Marc: How would you define yourself?*** Johnny: I continually struggle with this. When filling out passport applications. Every time I fill out a marriage certificate. When making studio name badges. For a while I started to get delusions of grandeur. I really started to feel that I was a director. In reality, I am emphatically a graphic designer. I make graphic images. My work, albeit moving image, is informed by graphic design. The label graphic designer should encompass all of these terms and definitions. A designer will shoot on 35mm. The term 'motion graphics', which I loathe, is for me completely redundant, some kind of mid-nineties anachronism. *Of course* graphic design moves. The beauty of graphic design today is that its practitioners approach filmmaking and animation with a completely different set of sensibilities. We are all familiar with how directors approach cinema. We've seen it for a hundred-odd years. Frankly, I've enjoyed shadow puppetry more than most cinematic output. If I want to see the world as it is, I can take a walk, or look out of my car window. The beauty of graphic design in any context is its superior ability to deliver remarkable visual metaphors in an original manner

that enables people to think or approach something differently. I know it's stating the obvious, but it's so easy to forget this. The relationship between graphic design and fine art is where it gets really tricky for me. Many fine artists would insist there is none, and I'd be inclined to agree, because graphic design is a language that the majority of people can read, if not speak. In my mind graphic design has the greater capacity to communicate, to touch and to change, and is marginally less obsessed with itself. ***Marc: When did you start working with moving images? How did you come to make* Phenomenon One?** Johnny: In '99 I started to think about making some of my 'bedroom' drawings move. I started to realise this might well be exactly what was missing. There was this long narrative strand developing in my sketchbooks, and I began to consider building a linear animation that would employ this. It was that simple. I had in my head The Beatles' *Yellow Submarine* film. I'd had no experience of animation and had no computer skills as such, but I worked it out and made it all in Photoshop. Once it was almost done, I contacted and persuaded the Freestylers to let me put a track of theirs across it, and that was it. It was a very speculative piece of work that I am now deeply embarrassed by. It's truly awful, but at the same time quite interesting. This rough test film was shown to PlayStation, and on the back of that, they commissioned the *History of Gaming,* which proved to be rather popular, but has

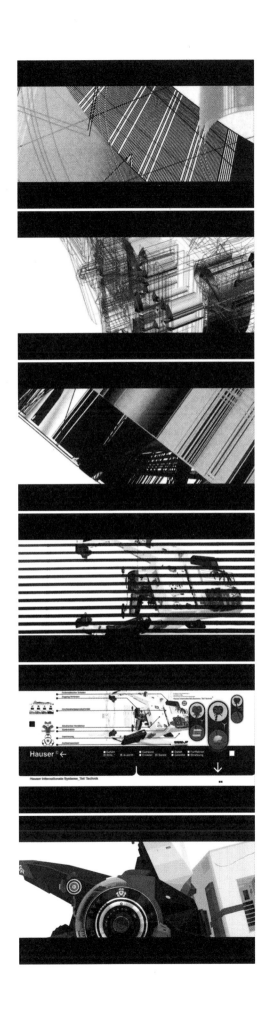

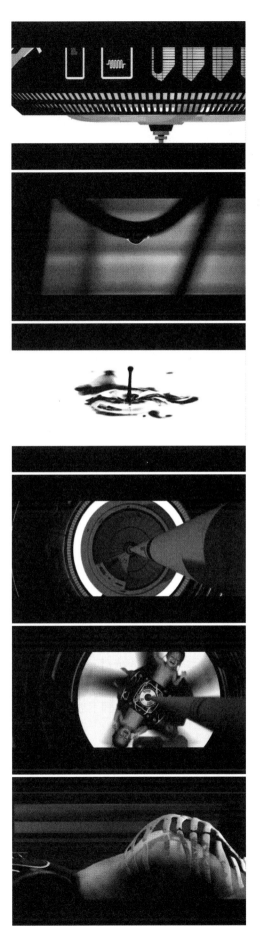

Radiohead Commission
2001–2002
Special commission by Radiohead/
Parlophone for tracks *Pulk/Pull
Revolving Doors* and *Like Spinning
Plates*

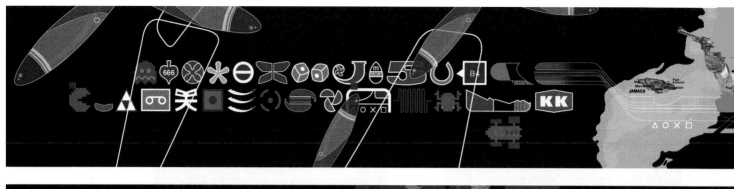

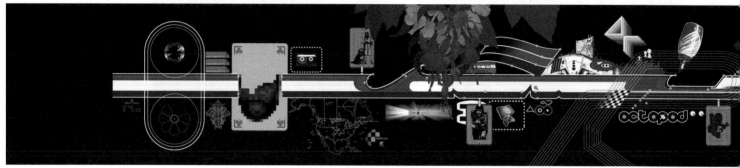

History of Gaming
1999
Commissioned by PlayStation

'I had accidentally got wind of an alleged internal-global conversation regarding a marketing disaster, so I decided to employ the corporate language of the conference call, and develop a conference call script that would truly question whether PlayStation is dangerous.'

the dubious honour of having spawned a thousand subsequent linear scrolling title sequences for Channel Five's endless *100 Best...* countdown programmes. Again, not a film I'm at all proud of.

Marc: In your work you seem to have a very personal agenda, how would you define it? Johnny: I have absolutely no idea. I think my agenda is loosely political. It may just be one huge problem with authority. I am horrified by inhumanity, in all its guises, by racism, fascism and war, by industrial manipulation and greed. I was born in the 1970s. Someone said to me recently that they felt that the Second World War didn't really end until the deluge of war films ceased in the mid-1970s. I agree. I have an odd love/hate relationship with the UK, with the monarchy, with tradition and modernity. With good and evil. I really don't know. I think that I am utterly preoccupied with what is underneath it all. With the truth. With disguise and decoration. Maybe my bullshit detector just runs at full tilt, and that's why I can't even listen to myself say these things without being deeply cynical with regard to myself. My rationale is simply to produce engaging, hopefully innovative work that actually says something in some way useful. ***Marc: What was the idea/inspiration behind* The Future of Gaming?** Johnny: *Future of Gaming* was a film I wanted to make regardless of who the client was. In many ways, looking back, I

had been deeply impressed by the economic/industrial power-play in Norman Jewison's original *Rollerball*. I knew that after making the *History of Gaming*, I could never make such a pointlessly fluffy film again, and I had it all worked out except for a narrative device to deliver the plot. When PlayStation approached me to make another film for them, the opportunity delivered an interesting narrative strand. PlayStation wanted another film. I was less than impressed with their leftfield marketing posturing. The suggestion, in their campaigns, that the PlayStation console was a 'dangerous' commodity. I felt it was 'dangerous', but not in the way they wanted it to be perceived. Personally, I think that gaming is very dangerous in that it sells false dreams and hopes and cheap empty escapism to countless force-fed consumers who get nothing back from their slavish compulsive gameplay and are short-changed of the one true commodity that we all have, which is time. It's hard enough growing up with serious prospects on an estate in some economically disadvantaged area, without some corporation encouraging you to devote all of your time to the limited imagination and personal shortcomings of some £50K a year programmer because you've been involuntarily selected as that corporation's core target. I had accidentally got wind of an alleged internal-global conversation regarding a marketing disaster, so I decided to employ the corporate language of the conference call, and develop

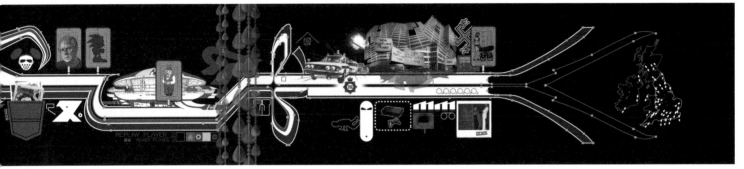

a conference call script that would truly question whether PlayStation is dangerous. I think its visual narrative arc, the Nazis and the Pope's penis and the endoscopic journey from a dog's mouth to its anus led PlayStation to distance itself from the film. It is one of the few projects that I made with which I feel a sense of satisfaction. Yet, ironically, whilst Playstation refused to have anything to do with the film directly, they were happy for me to exhibit it through film festivals and the like. Despite everything it made them look good. It made them look risqué. In that there is both the start of a new way of working and commissioning, and of course, some personal disappointment. **Marc: Are you particularly involved with computer games or game design?** Johnny: I can see their potential. I just cannot see how *Grand Theft Auto,* for instance, is in any way absorbing, useful or exciting. I love the notion of a virtual existence. I recognise just how absorbed we already are in virtual activities. But I like human interaction. I like physical experience. When computer games can entertainingly and quickly teach me Japanese, or make me leaner, fitter and stronger, or, best of all, simply overwhelm my imagination, then I will be their willing advocate, but contemporary gaming experiences seem to be written by people with very limited imaginations. I want more. Vast potential, but so far predictable offerings. Largely, gaming is based on sets of pre-determined experiences centred on less-than-fantastic

principles, however 'intelligent' and 'intuitive'. I think the word 'gaming' actually limits the medium. Perhaps if developers thought instead in terms of generating 'tender moments', for instance, rather than a game *per se,* then that could be fabulously engaging.

Marc: You worked with Radiohead, could you tell us a bit about that? How did it come about? Johnny: The Radiohead commission was very unusual in that it involved a high profile band on a big label letting me do just what I wanted. Dilly Gent had seen my *Future of Gaming* film and shown it to the boys, and I think they got quite into it. Initially I think the idea was to get me to look at making a promo for a major single release, but it quickly transpired that at the time I was not experienced enough as a director for that kind of undertaking. So instead, they asked me if I would like to choose a track, then offered to fund the production of a film for it. I couldn't decide between two tracks on the album, so I asked if I could take both, and fuse them together with an audio section of my own instigation. I wanted to cut the first track down, and strip Thom's lyrics out of it, and they agreed to everything. It was a case of them being remarkably free and generous. Through their commendable patronage, I managed to make an extended near-nine minute double music video. They didn't want to know too much about what I was going to do, and Dilly trusted me. Because the film involves

the surgical and industrial separation of conjoined twins, MTV were never likely to play it, but it achieved a life through DVDs and film festivals. *Marc: You have been involved with Mother and Orange. What about advertising work?* Johnny: I do very little advertising work, but I have a lot of meetings, and sometimes you do find yourself caught up in something you don't believe in, and then you have to extricate yourself from said projects by writing treatments based around Satanism and the Occult. I do think it's an interesting forum, and I find the political intricacies and dialogue that underpins it fascinating in its twists and turns, but working in advertising has never been an ambition in itself. The Orange job with Mother was a pleasing experience because it was such a very simple job, and wasn't spinning any deep conceit or unattainable lifestyle. Shooting flowing, overflowing paint is simply a very charming way to spend a couple of days. More like a pre-school activity than a high pressure job. The *Paint* film is interesting because it has no real narrative of any nature whatsoever. It's defiantly anti-narrative. Paint falling. End of. The agency asked for paint falling, and that was all I needed and wanted to give them. It really depends on the agency and the product. Sometimes, when both the agency creatives and the 'product' are very good, it's irresistible and you have to do the job. I feel like I should have a huge problem with advertising, but then I've always admired the way the Eameses interacted with commercial clients and industrial patrons, albeit in more optimistic times. Maybe it's just about being selective and gentle. The Orange ad is a good example of this, perhaps. *Marc: You do a lot of self-initiated work; do you also work with clients? If so, how do they react to your approach?* Johnny: Most of my work, whilst not seeming like it, is in fact for clients. I have a terrible tendency to doodle aimlessly unless there is the stark reality of some kind of 'commission'. I think it's a throwback to studying graphics. I am somewhat lost without a brief, however vague, but the minute I'm delivered one, I work ceaselessly to undermine it and reinvent it. This is of course nothing more than being contrary, a bit of a shit kicker, but I think it breeds good work, exciting, innovative work. It's my own motivation. I'm lost without something to kick against. It has to be a bit of a battle. Oddly, and somewhat frustratingly, people have bought into this, and actively expect it. But then that's my bluff being called. *Marc: Do you sometimes struggle to compromise money-making projects with more personal ones?* Johnny: I do have a problem with them, primarily because I just can't get that excited about money jobs. It's all very nice, and I do alright, but I don't see cash as the prime incentive.

This frustrates myself as well as others enormously. I've been very lucky in that I tend to get approached to make the work I want to make. I've taken a few money jobs, but on the whole, I'd rather not work at all than make work that I don't believe in. A year or so ago the financial agenda and the low-grade commercial ambition of others led me to briefly forget this. I see a new definition of 'graphic design' emerging. There are new ways of working, new opportunities, which ultimately involve graphic design being considerably more than just a means to making money. I'd rather genuinely push for this than opt for empty posturing and vague allusions to that in order to facilitate the making of a few pounds. From my deathbed, a high-end BMW and a few expensive tropical holidays are not going to satisfy me in quite the same way that perhaps that all too elusive, singular 'seminal' piece of work might do. Ideally I'd have the BMW, a tanned corpse and 'that' seminal piece of work, but I'm not greedy. I am never too happy with anything I make, but I can say for sure that the more money has been thrown at a project the less I have liked the end result. My agenda is to get paid for exactly what it is that I want to make, and some of my projects have been nothing more than experiments in doing just this. Some clients are more sophisticated now, more open to different models of commissioning, and I think what we are witnessing is industry moving, ultimately, towards sponsoring experimentation, which is both liberating and one enormous turn-on.

Marc: Your work seems to show particular interest in technique & science and its relationship to the human form. Do you have a particular interest in science? Johnny: It's about a love / hate relationship with technology, and an empathy for vulnerable people. Working in the mortuary, spending so much time amidst mostly old and invariably dead people does something to you. We live and exist in what is ostensibly a huge machine, and we are so hopelessly fragile. It was oddly comforting being a part of that process. I think it stops you fearing death and fosters a huge appreciation of time, a fascination with flesh and the body. Decay is very intriguing and utterly pervasive. If I think too long on the nature of the human body and its functions, I find myself questioning everything. Our necessity to consume only what is in the process of decomposition strikes me as unsettling, not to mention how it is virtually impossible to look at any crowded public space at lunchtime, or indeed anytime, without imagining the sheer quantity of faeces that these people are continually generating, gorging themselves on

Paint
2005–2006
Orange film, commissioned by Mother

'The Paint film is interesting because it has no real narrative of any nature whatsoever. It's defiantly anti-narrative. Paint falling. End of. The agency asked for paint falling, and that was all I needed and wanted to give them.'

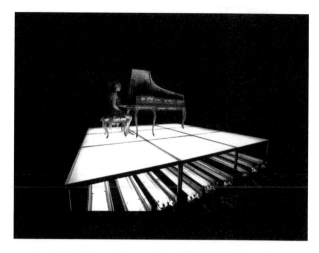

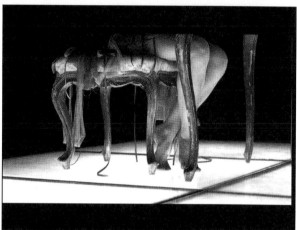

Hayling
2002
Mixed media music video for
FC Kahuna's track *Hayling*.

'I did for a while spend an inordinate amount of time at the Royal College of Surgeons, but I think that was more to do with me just liking the ambience of the place, as with the Veterinary College in Camden. I like that blend of academia and surgical spirit. There's something deliciously thoughtful yet brutal about it.'

acres of sandwich and then pumping it back into their environment as foul effluent. The individual is beautiful, sensitive, touching. The crowd feels parasitic. I have trouble identifying exactly how I really feel about humanity. All of this incubates itself in my sketchbooks in so many ways, and it tends to cross-pollinate, developing new strands and imagined scenarios and future prototypes, and quite often it gets expressed in scientific language. I am fascinated by science, and yet I am in many ways absolutely terrified of it, at least in the hands of mankind. I think most people feel this way.

Marc: How much of your work is done on a computer and how much of it is done by hand, in your sketchbooks? Johnny: Initially, everything I do is by hand. I find it essential to draw and plan virtually every aspect of what it is I'm trying to generate. I have no real love for computers. I'm a Luddite when compared to many designers. Hand-drawn images are desperately seductive, still the foremost means of explaining precisely what it is you want. I cannot imagine working any other way. I find that I can, on bigger projects, say where there is a team of people at my disposal, maintain more control and achieve exactly what I want by drawing everything out meticulously, like an engineering draftsman. There are projects for which I ended up producing a hand-drawn manual of sorts. Arguably the manual was nicer than the finished film. It is retentive, working this way, and it doesn't make you many friends, but drawing everything out is a good way of ensuring your vision is not diluted by various disparate agendas and the ambitions of others. You can generally tell which filmmakers or designers can't draw ... They tend to be less ambitious. *Marc: Do you do a lot of research?* Johnny: Because I am always developing my ideas and then applying them to projects in exactly the way that you are not supposed to, I don't tend to need to research things that I am already preoccupied with. I guess I'm continually researching the things that naturally fascinate me. I draw more inspiration from the broadsheets than anywhere else. There are times when I've felt the need to seriously bone up on something. I did for a while spend an inordinate amount of time at the Royal College of Surgeons, but I think that was more to do with me just liking the ambience of the place, as with the Veterinary College in Camden. I like that blend of academia and surgical spirit. There's something deliciously thoughtful yet brutal about it. I think most of my research interests were initiated as a child. My parents would take me around the country on a grand tour of Englishness. Museums. Galleries. Libraries. Stately homes. The

National Trust alone was responsible for a significant portion of my education. I wasn't too impressed at the time, but looking back, it was very formative. I do spend some serious time in the V&A's National Art Library, because it's a very inspirational place. Sometimes my research consists of nothing more than randomly stumbling around Google. Sometimes a tiny, distorted thumbnail is enough to trigger an entire narrative. I love that. I have always liked the way Hitchcock would have one simple scenario in his head, and from that simple image he would then work backwards to develop a complete and compelling narrative.

Marc: What are you working on at the moment? Johnny: I am working on a book project, which, upon completion, will have storyboarded a film I want to make. In a sense, what I am doing is making a graphic novel, only it's a graphic novel as I imagine the term 'graphic novel'. This narrative strand has been developing for many years, and I'm finding it all rather seductive. I've kind of realised that for me it's important to concentrate quite fixedly on one big project, and not get distracted by the smaller stuff. I've decided I would only make another film if it gets to be something that has intensity and purity and is free of censorship and commercial demands and agendas, rather than make lots of less substantial films as I could so easily do, and have done. *Marc: Do you work with a large team of people?* Johnny: I have been slimming things down. To such a point that now it's mostly just me on the book and film project. On commercial projects I have quite a loose collection of people I tend to bring in. There's an amazing 3D modeller and animator I work with sometimes. Paul can build anything I throw at him. There is a great physical model maker I love collaborating with. I'm constantly in awe of his skills. There is a great sculptress and a wonderful costume designer called Sam Perry who is very clever and accomplished. All these people are talented and good-hearted and atypical. On bigger commercial projects requiring studio or location shoots, with crew and producers and editors and sound designers and lots of Flame and CGI – by the time the film has been clocked you realise that what seemed like an initially simple project has probably employed a hundred people in one way or another. I like the alternating the scale of each project, and I've always been happy art directing, but at the core of it all, I like to be in control of every aspect and that level of control only comes on small jobs and personal projects. I admire the monastic model, spending a lifetime on one character in an illuminated manuscript. There seems a purpose in that. Do one

thing well, and do it sublimely. *Marc: You just had retrospective shows in Japan and Korea?* Johnny: I've exhibited work in some form or other quite a lot in Japan over the last four years. I adore spending time there, but the retrospective in Korea was a different experience. Of course it was a small affair, but it was good to see how a Korean audience reacted to work like mine. Korean people seem thoughtful and passionate, similar to, but maybe not as reserved as a Japanese audience. Japanese and Korean audiences have a far deeper appreciation of design work and design sensibilities. They look for and talk of spirituality within design, and I respect that very much. In many ways I felt fraudulent in that I don't, or don't think I do, ever consider that extra dimension. It's easy to be endlessly cynical from a western viewpoint about such things, but in comparison, we produce work in the west in a somewhat crass and bankrupt fashion. Experimental work is scarcer in Asia, but what there is, is far more experimental. It has very different sensibilities, and an aesthetic that we don't actually 'speak', and therefore can't assess. My exhibition had been arranged remotely, but I think it worked. I flew out there, and each night I was asked to hold a seminar. I screened additional work, and showed my sketchbooks and talked about my projects and related issues to an audience of Korean designers and students. The depth of their questioning struck me as unusually intense in comparison to English audiences. I completely fell in love with Seoul. As with Tokyo. I hate it when it's time to leave. The drive from Narita into Tokyo, considering Chiba is so grim, is just about my favourite thing. Full of potential. *Marc: Books, reading?* Johnny: I read voraciously and quickly. Novels, broadsheets, periodicals, manuals, anything at all really. It's the absorption of data and information. I like to re-read novels two or three times immediately upon completion just to be sure I have not missed anything salient. I hate the idea of overlooking an allusion, and I like to dissect narrative structures once I've got the complete picture. I find books desperately seductive. The act of appropriating them and consuming them. There is an early, self-published Hans Bellmer volume, individually hand scented very subtly with children's perfume. I adore that attention to detail. I spend a lot of time in the National Art Library at the V&A. It's really quite erotic. Miles of tightly bound knowledge, the scent of antiquated leather. I was tempted to pursue history and archaeology when I left school. I still have this rather crass, fawning love affair with academia. To an extent this shows within some of my work. *Marc: Does some of what you see around you in galleries and books end up in your own work?* Johnny: No. I really hope

Station launch film for BBC3
2002–2003
Commissioned by Fallon UK

'I like to re-read novels two or three times immediately upon completion just to be sure I have not missed anything salient. I hate the idea of overlooking an allusion, and I like to dissect narrative structures once I've got the complete picture.'

Mixed media promo for
Super Furry Animals
2001
Commissioned by Sony Records

'I'm interested in the past and the future. Not someone else's 'now'. It seems the emptiest moment, 'now'. You can feel a sense of competition in some people. You can smell it. I think it's really destructive.'

not. That's what I try to absolutely avoid. Obviously it can happen. No one is immune. Some things just do slip under the radar. But I try to avoid being infiltrated or infected. I purposefully never watch contemporary work. I never watch showreels, or look at what other people in contemporary design are doing. I think it's unhealthy. It's not out of ignorance. There is just never enough time in the day. I'm interested in what I can do, not what someone else is doing right now. I'm interested in the past and the future. Not someone else's 'now'. It seems the emptiest moment, 'now'. You can feel a sense of competition in some people. You can smell it. I think it's really destructive. They have to know what everyone else is doing. They rate their own success by others. I find that a bit ugly. They claim to be your 'competition'. We're not in a competition, and if we were, I'd be the judge of who my 'competitors' were. There's a scene for all that which I try to avoid. Certain obvious books have an unavoidable impact. Whilst it's regarded now virtually as a school text, *1984* informs everything I think about. It conjures up all that terrifies and secretly excites me. As much as I deplore fascism, in some ways its existence defines and galvanises us. I do find that a great deal of news and political thinking and economic data is readily absorbed in my work. I feel entitled to it. It's my existence. My daily life. I find the first fourteen pages of newspapers rich in inspirational triggers. As with the *New Scientist*. World financial news is always

fascinating in a morbid, fatalistic way, and yes, it all gets boiled down into some kind of odd synthesis. A good example of this is *The Future of Gaming*. I made it shortly before the Twin Towers attacks. The film features airliners dropping out of the sky onto US cities, extreme Arabic calls to arms and US military aggression, and in every way it is indicative of everything I was reading at the time of its making. I just didn't expect it to be quite so literally prophetic. I find it fascinating, the way current events subtly sway our collective psyche so imperceptibly at the time, but so dramatically in retrospect. ***Marc: What would you say are your most important influences?*** Johnny: I think the melting pot of childhood determines what you become most influenced and inspired by. For me it's a kind of synthesis of the toys I played with as a child, the absolute horrors that are perpetrated in warfare, punk, and an uncomfortable sense of Englishness. All of these things are part of it. Capitalism. Socialism. Heritage. Tradition. History. Science fiction. Nature. The English countryside. My home town. Eugenics. Genetics. Hans Bellmer. Orwell. The miners strike. Kurosawa. Foxgloves. Definitely Elem Klimov. Winsor McKay. Forests. Japanese crafts. Tokyo model shops. Bosch (not the power tool manufacturer – they're good, but I prefer Makita). It is quite frustratingly endless. It would help me enormously if I could narrow it down, but I'm really interested in so much. ***Marc: What are your ambitions?*** Johnny: My ambitions

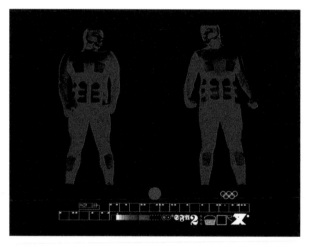

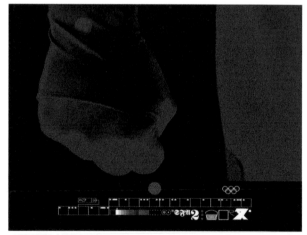

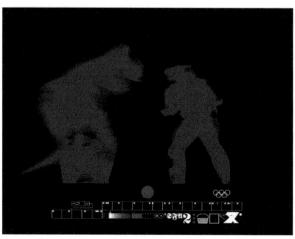

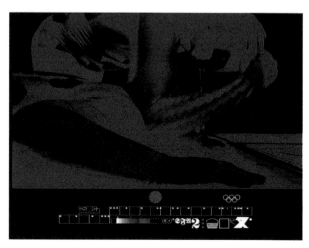

change daily. Since answering these questions, I'd half decided that I would love to make toys. Sometimes I feel like my head turns out good ideas just a little bit too fast and way too often. Overall, I would like to become more prolific and more studio-bound. If the book I am working on transpires to be as strong as I hope it will be, then I'll be happy. I like the way Svankmajer has always worked. Using materials and cast that come to hand to create extraordinary work. I'd love to have a studio or workshop in Tokyo. I like to find the time to teach at undergraduate and postgraduate level too, and I'd like to do that on a more intense level also. As a student at art college I never appreciated half-hearted educators, and I really subscribe to that Bauhaus notion of progress being initiated within arts education, not within 'industry'. Truthfully, I store ideas and potential projects up like squirrels store nuts. There are so many things I'd like to get moving on, but I'm learning to be much more selective now and have the confidence to say 'no' a lot more. In short, my ambition is to do more. More frequently. More varied, and more often. More print, more film, more innovative … and to make toys. Yes.

Marc: Let me now just ask you a few questions that relate to this issue in particular. How would you define your character? Johnny: Non-speaking. *Marc: Who's your ideal audience?* Johnny: I've always been fond of any audience that claps like seals and begs loudly for more. But ideally, my audience would be deeply intelligent, classy and quietly sexy women, preferably brunettes, in beautifully cut emerald green suits, who point softly at my work in gently lit, fusty bookshops, tip their head enigmatically, slide their glasses slowly to the tip of their nose and nod warmly at me. Is this a little too specific? *Marc: No, it's good. What's your kryptonite?* Johnny: Subtle variations on the following enquiries: 'Would Johnny be interested in a toothpaste commercial? No? It is watermelon flavour …' 'We're thinking of Johnny for this … It's a dancing Citroen … It's like a Transformer. No? It's different though. It bodypops … It moonwalks!' *Marc: And who are the good guys, who are the bad guys?* Johnny: Generally you can tell them apart by the monochromatic shade of their Stetson. The good guys never work in marketing or PR. The bad guys, deep down, know exactly who they are. *Marc: What's the happy ending?* Johnny: In London a 'happy ending' is massage parlour slang used to describe a customer's eventual, and ideally for the masseur / masseuse involved, exceedingly premature, ejaculation. That has kind of stripped all of the romance out of the phrase for me. Don't even ask what a 'shiner' is. *Marc: No, I won't!*

* * *

www.johnnyhardstaff.com

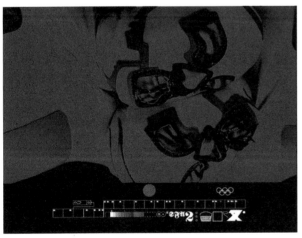

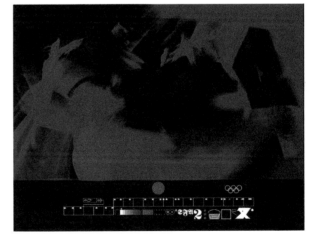

Kim Hiorthøy

The Deadline. Yes. Of
Course. The Deadline…
An interview with
Kim Hiorthøy

by Marc Valli

Right
Kim Hiorthøy

Far right
Oslo Cinematheque
07–08.2003
'I've worked for the Cinematheque
in Oslo for a number of years, first
doing their twice-yearly posters,
then the illustration for the cover
of their bi-monthly programme.'

**'I usually wait until the
last minute before I
start a job and then
work very fast. I don't
know why this is. It
never seemed to me
a very good idea. I'm
almost always late and
afterwards I feel that
the result would have
been better if I had
taken more time and
worked more on it.'**

The other day I opened the paper and read the
sentence: 'Understatement reminds us that there is
something under our statements.' This was not written
about Kim Hiorthøy. It happened to be an essay on
Freud, of all people. But I thought, *yeah, that's Kim
Hiorthøy alright.* Understated yet opinionated, at the
same time satirical, lyrical, vague, precise, poignant,
minimal, spontaneous, unresolved, insightful, deadpan,
often ostensibly unoriginal and yet completely new,
different, all over the place (using typography,
illustration, improvised sculptures, scribbles, words,
songs, recipes…) and yet contained, controlled,
instantly recognizable, unmistakably Kim Hiorthøy's.
His work is the perfect antidote to the day-to-day
grind of commercial graphic practice. There's always
warmth in the work. Behind every piece you guess
that there's a little story, a half-serious, semi-surreal
joke, a more or less coherent anecdote, a glimpse of
life. I like to imagine Kim as the flâneur of the graphic
world, wandering through the streets of Oslo, Berlin
and London with a cell phone and a Mac.

*Marc: How would you define yourself? Artist?
Graphic designer? Musician? Illustrator? Other?*
Kim: I've tried not to. Partly because I am a coward,
but also because not calling myself anything makes
it easier for me to do things. *Marc: What was your
first passion, I mean, in terms of artwork?* Kim: I
found out about Andy Warhol when I was around 15
and he became very important to me for a long time.
*Marc: You seem to do a fair bit of self-initiated work
– do you also work with clients? If so, how do they
react to your approach?* Kim: The only new clients I
get now are through my agents [This Is Real Art – see
questions on page 46] and they usually handle most
of the back and forth with clients, so to be honest I
don't really know. Outside of that I really only work
for people I have known for long time. I try to be
professional and reasonable, I suppose. It's mostly

a case of being asked to act in this or that capacity
and I try to respond accordingly. *Marc: I've always
wondered how your agents 'sell' you, or rather, how
they present you and your work to potential clients?*
Kim: I love my agents and I have a lot of respect and
humble feelings for them. I have no idea how they
present me and my work to potential clients. And I'm
happy that way.

Marc: Is there such a thing as a Kim Hiorthøy style?
Kim: Well there's the constant absence of any kind of
precision or elegance. A persistent lack of originality
perhaps, sad attempts to copy semi-old work by
M/M Paris, Tomato, The Designers Republic or other
famous designers. Pitiful emulations of whatever is
the flavour of the month. I would like to say I don't
have a style, but I probably do; just the sum of my
shortcomings and my limits and interests and habits
and so on. It gets tricky with styles, particularly
with getting work, where on the one hand it's good
for business if people can recognize your things and
want them, but at the same time you want to do new
things and not repeat yourself. *Marc: Tell us a bit
about your work methods.* Kim: It depends so much on
what type of project it is and who it is for, but almost
always when I am given a job I have some immediate
flash in my head of what it should be. I sometimes
try and follow that idea, but often worry that since
I thought of it first it's probably crap and I should to
try and think more, or just think of something new.
But often I also feel that trying too hard to think of
something new or 'original' or 'what it is' gets in the
way of what is really needed, if that makes sense, and
I should have just done the first thing that came to

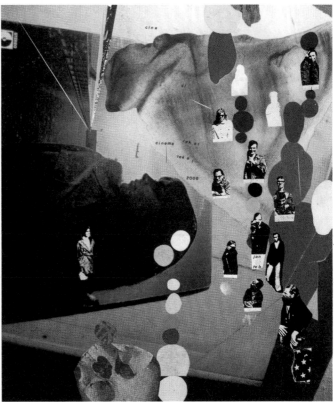

me. None of that made any sense, did it? To be honest I am not completely sure what my work methods are. The truest thing is perhaps to say that my only method is to just start working. A lot of ideas aren't articulated when I start working and instead I'll just start working and things happen as I go. I usually wait until the last minute before I start a job and then work very fast. I don't know why this is. It never seemed to me a very good idea. I'm almost always late and afterwards I feel that the result would have been better if I had taken more time and worked more on it. I don't really make sketches or roughs, I usually just begin on the thing itself. Although sometimes things can benefit from being made fast. *Marc: Do you work in a 'studio'? Do you work with other people or hire assistants?* Kim: I've always worked at home, or lived in the place where I worked. I tried to have a separate places for living and working for a while but I just ended up spending all my time in the place where I worked. I like to be able to work whenever I want, without having to consider when to be at work or when I need to go home to eat or sleep; or to have to consider what I have to bring with me home or back or which books and records stays in what place etc. I also like to go back and forth a lot between work and doing other things (what, I suppose, is also known as 'lack of discipline' or 'not really concentrating on the task at hand'). For these reasons I've also never had an assistant or felt that I could take an intern.

Marc: Your work always seems to be full of spontaneity, yet at the same time, when one looks at your work more carefully, it becomes clear that you think about it in very precise and original terms. It seems that your work is always balanced on that fine line, between intellectual and spontaneous responses to something. How do you keep that going? How do you make that happen? Kim: Thank you for saying all that. I don't know, to be honest. Or, as I mentioned earlier, I do often follow the ideas that come first, perhaps some feeling of spontaneity can come from that. Sometimes being past the deadline forces you to be spontaneous and that can make you do things you otherwise wouldn't have come to. But I often think that I'm trying too hard and that things feel contrived, and often afterwards I feel that I should have thought about the work more, been more precise. *Marc: Once you've been handed a commission, let's say an album cover, what do you do? Do you go out for a walk?*

Light a cigarette? Kim: Yes, sometimes. I usually feel self-congratulatory and then put off actually doing the work until the last minute. It would probably be better to work first and feel good later. But getting a commission is always a good feeling, always exciting and takes away whatever resentments I have with previous jobs. I don't mean to make this sound like I hate everything I do; I don't, but when I'm given a new job there's always a feeling of new opportunities and a chance to make something better than before. *Marc: Do you re-work a lot? Throw a lot away?* Kim: Yes. *Marc: Do you do a lot of research?* Kim: No. I should. I don't know if 'research' is the right word for it, but when I started out it felt like so much was going on around me with graphic design and there were so many things I wanted to do. This has changed over the years as I've worked and I don't get excited in the same way any more and I have had to start looking in other places. I try to have a 'beginner's mind' when I start a new project but it's not as easy as it used to be. I have more history, which is a resource for sure but also can weigh you (me) down.

Marc: How much of your work is done on a computer? Kim: Some work ends up there, but only at the very end. Some begins there. Most starts on the table and gets worked in by and by. Everything usually has to be finished there. *Marc: Do you read a lot? What do you read?* Kim: I buy a lot of books. I am obsessive about going to bookstores and can easily spend days in them. I used to read magazines but they always made me feel like a loser, so I stopped. I don't have a TV and like to read newspapers. I buy novels but will read several at a time and end up not finishing any of them. I am better at non-fiction, which I probably read more, and which is also often better suited for picking up at random. *Marc: Is music an important factor? Do music and visual artwork connect? Feed off each other?* Kim: Music is very important, but I don't know about connecting the music and art so much. I've never liked record sleeves where I felt that they tried to 'illustrate' the music. I don't think there's any need for it. Things feed off each other anyway and in ways you can't control and can often be more exciting the less you try to control them. *Marc: Who are the people who most influenced you?* Kim: You mean people I have known personally? My parents always told me to draw when I was a kid. That influenced me, I think. I spent a lot of time alone

Opposite page
Oslo Cinematheque
2004–2006
Covers of the Oslo Cinematheque bi-monthly programme.

Top left
May / June 2005

Top right
January / February 2004

Bottom left
July / August 2005

Bottom right
January / February 2006

'I like to be able to work whenever I want, without having to consider when to be at work or when I need to go home to eat or sleep; or to have to consider what I have to bring with me home or back or which books and records stays in what place, etc.'

Geir Gulliksen
HVIS JEG MÅ VÆRE MEG
Dikt 1995-2005

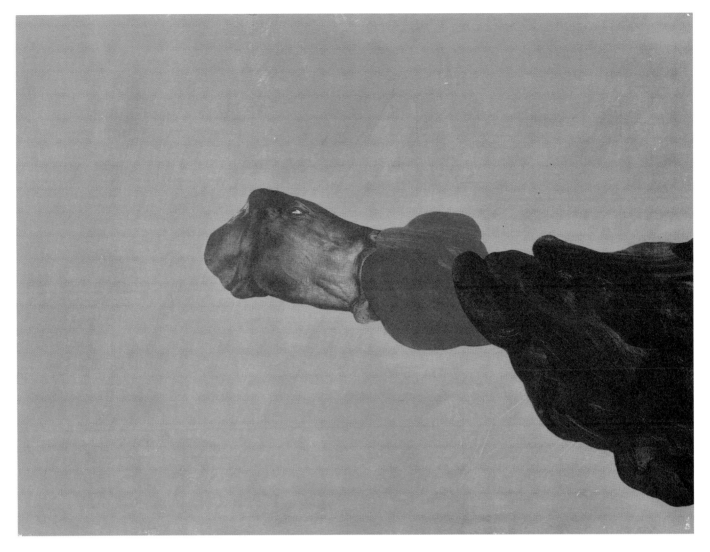

Opposite page
Geir Gulliksen:
Hvis Jeg Må Være Meg
2005
Book jacket for Aschehoug
Publishers, Oslo.

Above
Untitled
2004
Collage from the show at
No.5, Bergen Kunsthall.

Left
Untitled
1999
Drawing from the show of
300 drawings, Oslo.

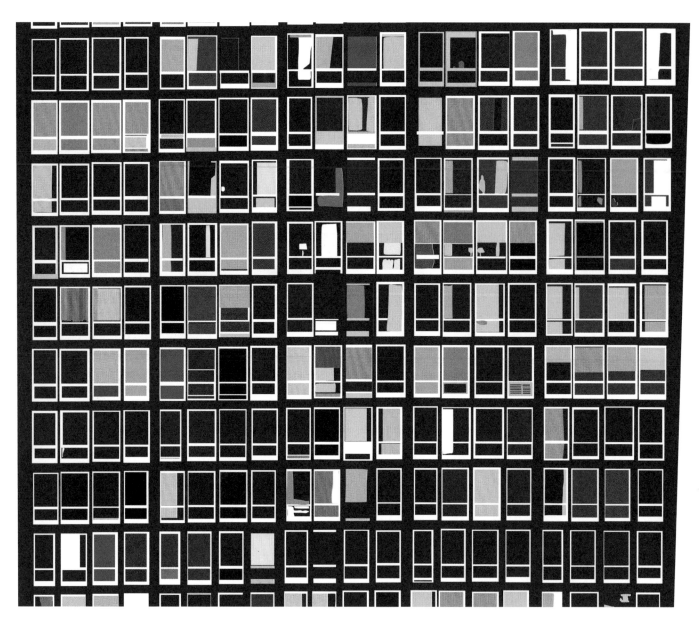

'Friends have taught me a lot. People I've worked with. If you know someone well and you know how they work, it can be good to ask yourself how you think they would approach something and then try and do that.'

growing up. It wasn't until I was in my mid-twenties that I met people I felt I could really learn something from. Friends have taught me a lot. People I've worked with. If you know someone well and you know how they work, it can be good to ask yourself how you think they would approach something and then try and do that. I sometimes do this with people I haven't seen in years. I like that you can keep the experience of someone with you in this way. *Marc: I meant more as in which other artists (or figures) inspired you most as an artist?* Kim: Other than Warhol, the figures and artists who have influenced me on and off, in kind of chronological order from circa 1989 would be (among others, these are the ones I can think of now) Dave McKean's drawings for *Violent Cases*, Bill Sienkiewicz's drawings for *Elektra*, Vaughan Oliver / 4AD, Fabien Baron, David Carson, Martin Venezky, various people I read about in *Emigré* magazine early to mid-nineties, Robert Frank, early William Wegman,

Reid Miles for Blue Note, Ben Drury / Mo'Wax, Shinro Ohtake, William Eggleston, Mark Rothko, Ellsworth Kelly, Ed Ruscha, the Edward R. Tufte books, Tom Friedman, Agnes Martin, and young graphic designers Grandpeople and Yokoland.

Marc: I was told that you were working on another book, is that true? How far are you? What kind of book is it? Kim: There might be a follow up to *Tree Weekend* if I can get it made. *Marc: Recently you designed a series (in fact more than one series) of t-shirts for This Is Real Art. There was one in particular, which unfortunately was not produced, but which intrigued everyone. It was a blue figure. I thought it was a ghost, but everyone seemed to see a different thing in it. What was it, in fact?* Kim: It was a picture of a boa constrictor digesting an elephant, my Drawing Number One. *Marc: I think you are now based in Berlin. Why Berlin?* Kim:

TODAY: NOTHING

Opposite page
Mies
2002
'Illustration. I was asked by Hans Seeger to do something for an edition of *Big* magazine which he was editing, I think, and which should have something to do with Chicago. I tried to do something about Mies van der Rohe's Lake Shore Drive apartment buildings but lost my confidence and never sent it.'

This page, top left
Poster for Magma
2005
'One of three posters from the show we made.'

This page, top right
A boa constrictor digesting an elephant
2005
'Made for the TiRA-commisioned T-shirts.'

This page, left
Various Artists: Money Will Ruin Everything
2003
Kim Hiorthøy, Rune Kristoffersen (ed)
'Early spread from the 5-year Rune Grammofon anniversary book / double CD, showing images for slides to accompany a Rune showcase tour of the UK in 2003.'

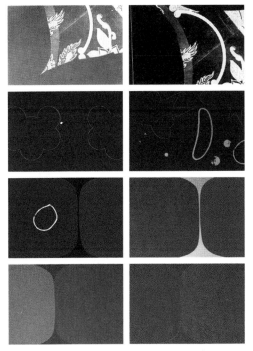

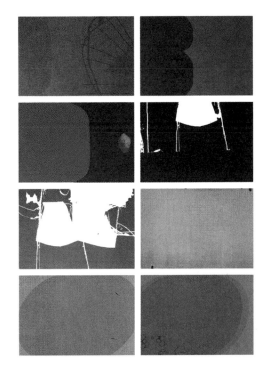

In 2003 I was offered a stipend to go and work or study anywhere I liked in Germany (it was a German stipend). I rented a flat in Berlin and ended up keeping it after the stipend was up. I've kept my studio in Oslo and now go back and forth.

Marc: When we organized an exhibition of your work we had to delay it as you were acting in a musical back home? Is that right? Tell us a bit about it? Kim: Not really a musical, it was a dance performance and it was in Sweden (not Norway). Director / choreographer Gunilla Heilborn had used my music for a dance film and was directing another one and asked if I wanted to come and write some music during filming. I said ok, but that I then wanted to be in the film. So I ended up kind of dancing in her film, which she then made a follow-up performance for at the House of Dance in Stockholm and since I was a character in the film I was cast in the performance

also. We did seven shows I think, and we will do a small tour of Sweden in april this year. It was very strange and kind of interesting.

Marc: Let me now just ask you a few questions that relate to this issue in particular. How would you define your character? Kim: [makes vague gesture with hand] *Marc: Who is your ideal audience?* Kim: Animals. *Marc: What's your kryptonite?* Kim: Revenge. *Marc: Who are the good guys, who are the bad guys?* Kim: The blind. *Marc: What's the happy ending?* Kim: Nothing ends.

* * *

Left
***I love you but I have
chosen darkness***
Drawing / collage for a show at
No.5, Bergen Kunsthall
'I never studied graphic design
but fine art at an art school, and
lately have been doing more and
more art-art, through my gallery
Standard in Oslo and in other
places.'

Below
***Blood
Pinch***
2005
T-shirts commissioned by
This Is Real Art

Bottom
Moha! Raus Aus Stavanger
2006
Record sleeve, Rune Grammofon

'Kim is Kim. We can't dress him up into something he's not. But the funny thing about him is that he's not frightened of working with corporate or ad agencies. So, we talk to people quite freely about him. We never try to make him into something he's not'.

The Corporate Kim:
Questions to This Is Real Art.

Selling Kim Hiorthøy's style – or 'non-style' – to corporate clients did strike me as quite a challenge, so I decided to ask his agents, This Is Real Art, a bit more about it.

Marc: Did you first approach Kim? Why? TiRA: We've known Kim for a long time, and we're all fans of his work. He'd be very embarrassed to hear this, but he's also an exceptionally decent human being and very easy and rewarding to work with. In an earlier incarnation, before TiRA became a virtual design studio, the company sold original prints online, and Kim was one of the artists whose work was featured. *Marc: How do you sell him to a client?* TiRA: Well, Kim is Kim. We can't dress him up into something he's not. But the funny thing about him is that he's not frightened of working with corporate or ad agencies. So, we talk to people quite freely about him. We never try to make him into something he's not. *Marc: When do you think, yes, that is a Kim job?* TiRA: People react very strongly to his work. If they don't want to work with him, they say so very quickly. But

when potential clients respond well to his work, you know that he's going to be able to work with them. We had an instance recently when the manager of a well-known musician had an ecstatic response when he saw Kim's work – but when the musician saw it, he hated it. So, two extreme responses from the same client! *Marc: How do you get him to deliver work on time? Does that ever happen?* TiRA: Kim is busy all the time. He works on his own personal projects, on his music, and on projects for friends. But when he takes on a commercial project, he's totally focused. Obviously, this is where the TiRA structure can help – we can make life a bit more streamlined for him. But he always delivers – even if it's right up to the wire.

Marc: What was the idea behind the Factory Films identity? TiRA: Dilly Gent was our client on this. Dilly is a very sussed person. She knew that to get the best out of Kim she had to allow him to be himself, and in return, he delivered a solution that was very smart and understated. Factory had considered commissioning something rich and expressive, but they liked Kim's understated response; it allowed the music video directors that Factory represent to shine,

46

and it had a real graphic personality that over time would come to express Factory. Kim's solution took into account budgetary considerations, too. It was not a production heavy solution – which was part of the brief. *Marc: How did people at Fashion Week respond to the invite?* TiRA: Kim did a lot of quite polished ideas to start with, but at the last minute he threw in a sketch as a suggestion for another idea. His plan was to work the idea up, if it was liked. But the client loved it as it was – a scribble with hand lettering. Maybe they thought it was like a fashion designer's preliminary sketch? We had to convince Kim not to change it.

Marc: In what context was the MTV work produced?
TiRA: The brief was to produce 'sonic-idents' for MTV. In other words, they didn't want to use the MTV logo, instead they wanted to hear the words MTV. The reason Kim's pieces work is because of the audio. The animation is very basic (and all the better for that) but the sound design is genius. This is where Kim's work as a musician is so useful. Only someone skilled with sound could have made these pieces. Again, they were test pieces – but MTV approved them as finished pieces. We had to urge Kim not to tart them up; their strength is their rawness. They were approved without changes.

Marc: What's your favourite work by Kim Hiorthøy?
TiRA: I suppose it's his work for the Norwegian record label Rune Grammofon. It's a brilliant piece of sustained graphic expression. It's got everything – continuity but also diversity. And now, after a few years, there's a lot of it. Very few labels are this disciplined in terms of the commissioning process. Normally labels panic after a few releases, and change tack. Rune Kristoffersen, the label's owner, has shown amazing vision to stick with Kim and allow him to develop a really major body of work.

*   *   *

To celebrate its first year of existence, TiRA has commissioned a series of t-shirts. They include two of Kim's designs, *Pinch* and *Blood*, both £30

www.thisisrealart.com
www.smalltownsupersound.com

Below
Nils Økland, 'Bris'
2004
Record sleeve, Rune Grammofon

Bottom
Food, 'Last Supper'
2004
Record sleeve, Rune Grammofon

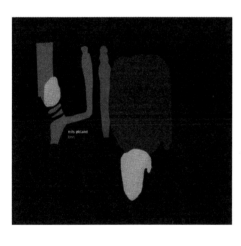

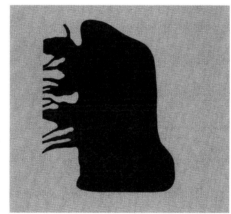

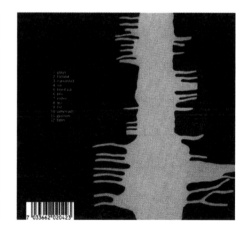

Gideon Ponte

The Story of The Shunned Girlfriend: An interview with Gideon Ponte

by Richard Brereton

For a number of years Gideon Ponte has worked with many leading fashion photographers, including the likes of Steven Meisel and Mario Testino, but he's perhaps best known for his work as production designer on movies such as *Buffalo '66* **(1998),** *Bongwater* **(1998),** *American Psycho* **(2000),** *Hamlet* **(2000),** *Series 7: The Contenders* **(2001),** *Abandon* **(2002),** *The Dangerous Lives of Altar Boys* **(2002),** *The Notorious Bettie Page* **(2006) and** *Nacho Libre* **(2006). I spoke with Gideon at his home in Tribeca, New York.**

Gideon: Hold on. Eli, no! Do not squirt me with that thing! Eli: Goofball! Gideon: Eli, I'm not joking, do not squirt me with that gun! I'm on the phone with Rich. I'll be with you when I've finished. Now go and play with your brother. I'm closing the door now, Eli. Do not come in here. I mean it, Eli!

Richard: Begin by telling me what a production designer does. Gideon: You organize, hiring the art department, setting them to work to meet the needs of the production, basically figuring out the script, breaking down the script, trying to realize the director's vision. Getting to work practically. Putting that into action. This means providing drawings and blueprints for the construction crew so they can start cutting wood and building. That's one thread. Then you've got instructing the scenics in terms of finish and at the same time the decorating department responsible for the small and larges: the furnishing, curtains, furniture, carpets and bits and pieces. In addition, you've got the prop department, which are responsible for anything that comes into contact with the actors. At the same time all materials on a movie need to be cleared, every cover of a book, every can of beans in a supermarket, every photo, picture, painting, sculpture, graphic all needs to cleared, paid for and signed off on.

In one way movies are much closer to a Edward Hopper painting or something like that. Partly because clearance is such a pain, partly because compositionally it's more interesting. If you look at Hopper's paintings they're stark. There isn't a bunch of belongings or signage. Is that because it didn't exist, or was it because he didn't want it in the first place? *Richard: So how did you begin working in films? What was your first movie?* Gideon: I began because Mary Harron was making *I Shot Andy Warhol*. It was

> *'You try and ask questions. Try and give answers. You kind of feel out what you, and they, are interested in.'*

her first feature and she was worried that the majority of films about making art or artists seem to get it wrong. She thought I might be able to help because of my background in the art world. While Therese DePrez was the production designer, I started doing research, which is often how you start. I found the original magazines Warhol took his images from. I then created silkscreens and made replicas of the paintings. After the filming, the Warhol Foundation came down to make sure we destroyed the paintings. *Richard: How do you get hired for a movie nowadays?* Gideon: I have an agent. The agent is pushing you around. The producer will have a project. Possibly meet five designers they like the look of. They send you a script to read. For me, conversation can be a little abstract so what I like to do is produce a look book. I respond to the script. Some directors' interests lie in the chemistry, the relationship between the characters. Some are extremely particular about the visuals. You try and ask questions. Try and give answers. You kind of feel out what you, and what they, are interested in. And something either works in that relationship or it doesn't. *Richard: When discussing the way a film looks, do you have to steer?* Gideon: Yeah. Most

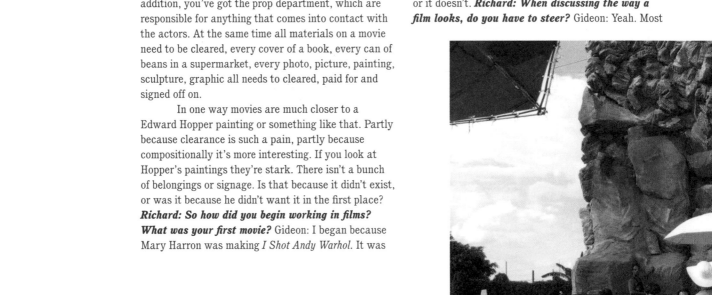

people know it when they see it but can't describe it. That's my job, filling in the blanks. Sometimes it's written on the page as if it's describing something you've already seen. I like to give the director as much information as possible; this can be blueprints, models, photo collages or taping out the set on the stage floor so they know what they'll be getting. Then there's the practical side, how you are going to achieve the shot.

On the last film I designed, *Nacho Libre* (2006) directed by Jared Hess, a comedy about luchadores – Mexican wrestlers – there was quite a lot of stuff going on. Special effects. We had to build an arena that could seat fifteen hundred people. I wanted the bleachers to be the background for the action in the ring. So in order to achieve this we had to build the bleaches much steeper and closer to the ring than you would in real life. Just the logistics of getting the rigging, camera, crane and that many people in and out is quite difficult. *Richard: Did you actually have fifteen hundred people?* Gideon: No. Five hundred. Plus five hundred rather creepy inflatable extras that we shipped in from L.A.

Richard: What excites you in a script: the narrative or the look? Gideon: Narrative, always narrative. Can I get into it? Getting excited is the thing. I don't know if there's a thread I'm learning, realizing. I get excited by period stuff for some reason. I don't know why. I think I like having that ground under me. I like digging into material, trying to find images from places that people haven't looked before, or have chosen to discard. That might be a weird catalogue from a restaurant, a cigarette pack, anything that holds my attention. Some designers are interested in colour palette. Others, design. I like visual material. *Richard: So you're taking visual material and putting it into a context within the script?* Gideon: Yeah. Maybe it's the fear. Fear of getting it wrong that's driving it. I'm not sure. *Richard: Is there a lot of fear?*

Gideon: Less so now. There's always an element in films that's string and tape. It's not real. This comes back to limitations. And what one needs in order to make an idea. Play around with an idea. You need to decide what it is you're dealing with in terms of visual language, style, period, materials, colour palette. Once you have defined that world, you can then decide if you want to break it. You need those limitations.

On *The Notorious Betty Page* (2006) there was huge amount of material, I think she was the most photographed model ever. Far more than Marilyn Monroe. In the end it comes down to what defines Betty Page. *Richard: You also work a lot in fashion?* Gideon: Yeah. For two years before *Betty Page* I was working with Steven Meisel. Learning from him. He's amazing. He's like a method actor. I mean, if doing a shoot based on a black and white Italian movie, which he might do, someone shows him a movie and he loves it, he's gonna have the Italian music. He'll keep his people helping him take the photographs very close to him on set. He's going to be extremely hard on himself and he's pretty much non-verbal. There's a performative element; by 'performative' I mean that when you're making a film or a photograph

that's going to be seen in a magazine or on screen, you also have the experience of making it. And that's the other side. You're with a bunch of people standing around in silence while others are doing something. I'm not saying there's always a relationship between performance and the making of a good photograph. But that's something that sometimes happens. That's interesting for me.

With Meisel, we'd have a meeting. He'd tell me what he wanted. He'd ask me to make a set. I'd try to do something to please him. He'd turn up on the day with his crew. He'd sit at his desk, edit the previous day's material. At that same time the guys are setting up the lights and we're setting up trying to get a feel of how the set will respond to the lighting. I can build a set but the amount of latitude by changing the lights is enormous. Plus there are huge variations of what scenic can do. Some are like master chefs. They turn up with recipes to make a craggy old wall which literally fools the eye. Then there is the shoot itself. The camera is a Cyclops. It only has one eye. It's not what the brain sees. Not what I see. It's in its own world. You're trying to anticipate how the camera might see your design.

'I like digging into material, trying to find images from places that people haven't looked before, or have chosen to discard.'

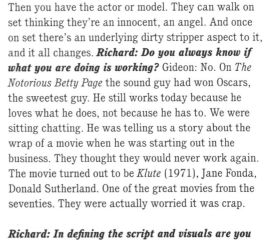

Then you have the actor or model. They can walk on set thinking they're an innocent, an angel. And once on set there's an underlying dirty stripper aspect to it, and it all changes. **Richard: Do you always know if what you are doing is working?** Gideon: No. On *The Notorious Betty Page* the sound guy had won Oscars, the sweetest guy. He still works today because he loves what he does, not because he has to. We were sitting chatting. He was telling us a story about the wrap of a movie when he was starting out in the business. They thought they would never work again. The movie turned out to be *Klute* (1971), Jane Fonda, Donald Sutherland. One of the great movies from the seventies. They were actually worried it was crap.

Richard: In defining the script and visuals are you always trying to find the essence, truth? Gideon: I worked with [Robert] Altman once on this weird commercial. He put it the best way. He told me two things: One, the idea of truth is: as soon as you're saying something is truth, it's like sand in your hands, it flows through your fingers. You have to muck around with this idea of truth that is elusive.

Another thing he said … well, he didn't say it, but I interpreted it from what he is doing. Here he is, an Oscar-winning director, who reinvented cinematic language through conversation. By trailing off a scene with conversations, pulling you into another scene with conversations, people talking over one another. You see his movies and you feel, 'I'm there'. Chaos. In fact it's not chaos. It's all carefully choreographed. His actors are like dancers. They have to hit their mark. He is going for something very formal and precise. Where he wants the camera to be. Where something is

being said. And you realize what it is that he is doing. He's setting himself a conundrum which he may not be able to think himself out of. He may not be able to solve this very complicated camera move in a small space with mirrors, people. But he is setting himself up in order to do something which he hasn't done before so he can think his way out of it. ***Richard: Is there a conundrum to solve on every film?*** Gideon: Often many. On *Nacho Libre* the director wanted one scene in one shot. The camera starts on the actor Jack Black with his sidekick tying a red cloak on his back. He then jumps over a fence into an enclosure. Jack Black's wiggling his bum and the bull enters, lowers his head and throws him in the air. That in turn becomes, 'how do we make this happen?' You've got the visual effects guy. You've got the camera department. The lights. Meanwhile you know the bull will not hit its mark. But this is the problem to fix. How to do it?

The director had in mind a fence you find on a farm. Then three weeks before shooting we sent the drawings to the animal wrangler and she comes back explaining we need a fence two metres high with timber sunk four feet into the ground. A bull fighting ring with barricades for the matadors to hide behind. Suddenly it becomes *Jurassic Park,* we go back to the producer explaining the cost will be $50,000 and it would make the shot impossible. How will Jack Black's character climb over the fence? Where will the camera be? We need to make a house for the camera. This is production design.

Richard: What happens when there are strong disagreements? Gideon: In short, people get fired. Typically, the DP [director of photography] comes

on late. In the eight weeks prior the director and production designer have discussed the design and discussed or seen most of the locations. At this point the director and designer are typically close. But when the DP comes on board you sort of get dumped. You're like the shunned girlfriend. It happens all the time. You get used to it. The production designer can become the scapegoat. But when things go really wrong, it's more likely the DP gets fired as they're easier to replace. The studio's unlikely to fire the director as the cost of closing down a production for a couple of weeks is too high. If you have a young director the producers or studio will usually balance that by getting an experienced DP who has the responsibility to make the days and to get the film in the can.

Generally, by the start of shooting the production designer has already done most of their work. I take the director round the set, which he may not have seen before. I try to give as much information as I can in advance. But you don't want to give them so much information that you haven't got something up your sleeve on the day. Something to say 'look' and for them to feel wow, I get to go to work today. ***Richard: What's the biggest thing you've built?*** Gideon: Not sure if there's a biggest. On *Nacho Libre* we built a convent. We made the choice of a long corridor with two rooms off it. One was for the sexy nun. Her room was upstairs, a pretty room with vaulted ceiling and a window, but all the other rooms we kept intentionally small. We didn't do the usual thing, build large then shrink in the camera. Often you build a room twenty-five by twenty-five and once you've added the camera, a dolly and the lights it's full and then the DP shoots close to the walls to give intimacy.

Instead, we built small with the ceiling rigged from above to lift off and the walls designed to be removed whilst making sure everything is attached to the walls so it can be removed quickly. All the

'When the director of photography comes on board you sort of get dumped. You're like the shunned girlfriend. It happens all the time.'

seams, the corners where it pops, where you split walls apart, were carefully hidden, so each time you remove the wall you don't need to repaint. It didn't make for an easy three days shoot, but it was an idea. You're in little tight rooms. And then when the film opens up and you're in big wrestling arenas and Mexican landscape. ***Richard: Has there been one build you're particularly pleased with?*** Gideon: Well, when you building a large structure like a monastery. First it's plywood. Then it becomes real. Then it becomes emotional. We built this! It's problem solving. The relationships between people. You don't do it all yourself. You work with lots of people to make it happen, getting the best out of your people, getting them excited. That's rewarding.

Richard: Which are the favourite directors you've worked with? Jared Hess was great. A 28-year-old Mormon, I don't know why he was so great. Partly, he never let it spin out of control. He never faltered. He went to church every weekend, had sense of fairness, enthusiasm, a belief in himself. Mary Harron's great to work for too. She's so smart, strong-willed. She fights for things. Vincent Gallo was amazing and crazy, an artist. He said there is a reality that we're interested in and then there's that additional thing. That's what the production designer does. The additional thing. Making movies is a slow process of building consensus. And at any point that consensus can collapse. At any point people can think 'this is crap'. It's all about trying to keep that sense of what you are doing. Although all too often, at some point sooner or later that faith goes. You think, 'what am I doing?' ***Richard: Are there such moments on every production?*** Gideon: Yeah. 'I don't know what I am doing. I don't have anything to offer. I don't know if what I'm offering is any good.' Yeah. That's all part of the process. The more you do, the more you recognize it. I also recognize friction is good too. It make things happen. Creativity. *Buffalo '66* was my first film. The first time you do it, you're making it up as you're going along, taking risks because you don't know any better. Maybe for me that's why filming in Mexico was so exciting. ***Richard: Where do you start sourcing materials?*** Gideon: Bookshops. I spend a lot of money on books. Probably $2,500 for each project. There are the obvious books which everyone has. On the last film we had three volumes of three inch files of just stuff. Sometimes obscure stuff from all over. It could be anything and slowly one starts to chuck things out, to build consensus.

Richard: What are your influences? Gideon: The great ones. *The Conformist* (Bertolucci, 1970). *Contempt* (Godard, 1963) They may sound a bit wanky, but they're amazing films. Also I have a couple of things that I go back to again and again – there's a weird book of Italian vampire photos from the seventies that I've been obsessed with for the last five years, I just love it. Then there's a Kippenberger book about furniture. ***Richard: In terms of your work, what are most pleased with and why?*** Gideon: Pleased with? I think it was the guy who started Artforum said you have a moment of apprenticeship, a moment of synchronicity and a moment of falling behind. In a career you probably have multiple moments like that. Often when you look at a production designer's work they may have one great seminal film then spend the next twenty years trying to make another.

I'm looking forward to *The Notorious Betty Page* and *Nacho Libre*. I don't know how they'll be received. I mean, look at *King Kong*. Everyone thought it would go through the roof. Then last week it was knocked off by a horror movie that cost four million dollars. You can never tell. ***Richard: Are you part of a scene?*** Gideon: No. I'm isolated. I do what I do. And I don't like anything I do. I just try and stay hungry. ***Richard: Do you hang out with film people, directors, talent?*** Gideon: No. That's above the line. I'm below the line. It's very blue collar, but I like it like that. ***Richard: Is fashion an antidote to features?*** Gideon: I like fashion because it's much smaller, more hands on. I like the intimacy. I'm about to do some fashion jobs again. I'm looking at the 1980s animation character Gumby. The colours are great. ***Richard: I can hear the boys screaming. I'd better let you go. Thanks for talking.*** Gideon: No problem.

* * *

'Vincent Gallo said there is a reality that we're interested in and then there's that additional thing. That's what the production designer does. The additional thing.'

Yan & Luke

An interview with Yan Elliot and Luke Williamson

by Richard Breretou

How do you sell crap in a sack? The answer: tell the truth. I met with award-winning creative directors Yan Elliot and Luke Williamson at the Century Club in London to discuss their house style: wit.

Richard: Tell me how you both got started in the advertising industry. Yan: I decided I wanted to be creative. I went to do a two-year course for art direction & copywriting at Watford College. You do that course, put a portfolio together and then you literally knock on the doors of agencies around town and see if anyone is interested in hiring you. Luke: I was a graphic designer, got a college degree, worked as a junior, worked as a practising designer, then helped out a friend who works at an ad agency with a pitch over one weekend. I thought it was really easy. I was freelancing at the time, and ended up sticking around for three months thinking it was quite a lark. It didn't have a lot of the restrictions and it was quite immediate which appealed to me. Mother (the ad agency) had just started, and I was doing bits and bobs for them as a freelancer. After a while Yan said 'come and be my partner'. Yan: I was working with a guy at Mother at that time who wanted to go off directing in the States. Just as Luke was starting to freelance at Mother, my old partner Jim Hosking decided to leave. So it was perfect timing.

'What does a creative director do? Shout at people all day. Have massages all afternoon'

Richard: Tell me what a creative director does. Luke: Shout at people all day. Have massages all afternoon. Well, it's very important for us to still generate work. So we still write and think of concepts and all that sort of thing, like a normal team would. But we also make sure everyone else's work is up to scratch. *Richard: Do you pitch briefs or do the briefs come to you?* Luke: Normally a brief comes into the agency from a client for a certain bit of activity. We all sit down to decide who works on what. *Richard: How many are in your teams?* Luke: Traditionally, a creative team is just two people. In our department there are nine teams. *Richard: Are you pitching briefs to clients or are clients coming to you with a product and then asking you to develop a pitch*

for them? Yan: A bit of both really. For example, Mini, an existing client, will be launching the new Mini. They will come to us and we'll discuss that brief. At the same time, there is the new business side of the agency, which is looking for new clients. We will be trying to court and pitch new business. Luke: Sometimes you get clients saying, 'we've got a problem, we want to do this, we want to sell X'. Your job is to verify if that self-diagnosis is true. Often you have to go back and say, 'that isn't the problem. The problem is over here, and you need to pitch it like this'. With the right client it can be a really good process, trying to get the best solution for the business. *Richard: What is the right kind of client?* Luke: Somebody who recognizes their business problem and wants to solve it in the most interesting way… Yan: Yeah. Also, a client who recognizes that they've come to an advertising agency because they're experts in advertising and marketing and doesn't believe that they can solve the whole problem themselves. *Richard: Do all clients recognise that?* Yan: No. Some clients think they know the solution and they just want you to execute it. They are the worst kind. The best ones are the most questioning ones, the ones that want to work with you as a team. The agency and the client should be one team solving one problem and it shouldn't be about us and them.

Richard: With Super Noodles did they come to you? Luke: Actually, they came to us saying that they have a potato substitute which gives more time for mum to spend with her husband and children. Yan: 'So please advertise it as a starch substitute to have with your lamb chop and peas.' Luke: We said that the starch substitution concept is not the true essence of the product. We think that Super Noodle is for people who are extremely lazy, who can't be arsed and are probably half drunk. 'It's toast, it's not toast. It's Super Noodle!' Yan: It's emergency food. You always have it in your cupboard. You eat it at eleven thirty at night. It's for blokes who are basically pissed from the pub. *Richard: Did the client accept that?* Luke: Yeah, they did. They're a brilliant client. That's Paula Quazi at Unilever. She instantly recognized that that was the truth. Yan: That's an example of a great client. I mean a lot of people think 'my product is so wonderful I don't really have to do much, everyone must love it,' and the truth is quite a bitter pill to swallow. If you tell them that actually their food is just nosh food,

crap in a sack, I think we called it at the time. The reality is, it's just not that glamorous, so we need to be honest about this thing. Don't pretend it's something it's not. Otherwise people say, 'that's not the Super Noodles I know'. It's very important to be true to the brand. Luke: That is the way we approach most things. What's the truth about the product? What's the truth about the brand? That will help you find the problem quicker and to find the solution. *Richard: What about if, for example, the product ain't all that? I mean, margarine is margarine.* Yan: You will probably find as well that the brands or products that seem less glamorous and don't have great advertising at first are the ones that do the best advertising later, because they're the ones that need to take the chance. There's less for them to lose. You will find a lot of hilarious ads for products that are quite small. They don't have the money so they have to make an impact. Luke: Also there's not the organizational politics, the logistics that can happen in an organization of two hundred people. The fewer people involved, the better. Yan: Yeah, and they are less scared too.

Richard: When you are brainstorming for ideas, is there a common ground where ideas stem from? Luke: I don't think so. Ultimately it's 'what do you want to say?'. We go out a lot and sit in coffee shops and talk. We go through a hell of a lot of thinking and discussing and usually the ideas come in the down-time, after you filter out all the crap. After a while, you look at the problem from a different angle and it becomes much clearer. Yan: Yeah, you look at the truth of the product, then work out what you're going to say about the product, and then what's the best way of saying that. You're always storing up things that one day you might be able to use.

Richard: Are you a tag team, or are you arguing? How does the brainstorming work? Luke: We feed off each other really. One person says one thing, the other person builds on it or kills it. Yan: One of us puts on the cement, the other puts on the brick, cement, brick, brick, cement. *Richard: Is that a touchy dynamic to deal with?* Luke: Not at all. Yan: No, but I think it can be for others. Certain creative teams I know hate each other. They won't socialize together. Won't do anything together. They just work together. I think the best creative teams are friends; thick as thieves, almost. It's hard to turn on just when you're at work. It might

'Certain creative teams I know hate each other. They won't socialize together. They just work together. I think the best creative teams are friends; thick as thieves, almost'

be quite nice to mention a thought when you're having a beer. We do deal with things differently, but we try to have a laugh. Luke. We have different social backgrounds. Different reference points. We look at problems and we look at solutions differently. But we are unified in the fact we like to work. We enjoy it. We like to make good work and have fun. ***Richard: Do you ever think the other person's idea is bad?*** Luke: All the time. But we let the other person live with the thought. And at some point, every time, one of us will say, 'this doesn't feel right'. Yan: Yes, it becomes apparent that something is not right. Equally when there's a great idea, everyone thinks is a great idea straight away.

Richard: How long do you have to come up with an idea? Luke: We prefer a shorter time period, two or three weeks. Yan: Sometimes you might have to come up with an idea over a weekend. ***Richard: What inspires you in the industry?*** Yan: Probably outside the industry, really. People, mainly people. What makes people tick? We don't do big extravagant visuals, you know, like yachts on the horizon with a sunset. Luke: Storytelling and narrative. We are interested in people and their relationships. ***Richard: What work of yours are you most proud of?*** Luke: Probably the Orange Cinema campaign. Yan: We were given a brief for a spot that says you've got five seconds to turn your phone off in the cinema. Then we noticed that Orange were running a sixty second ad beforehand and that they were also running that ad on the television. So we thought 'let's take those spots as well'. Luke: The cinema's a literate audience. Why not talk to them? Yan: Orange were up for that, so it was great. We would never usually use celebrities in advertising, but we've used them in a kind of anti way. The celebrities get dissed. Luke: The truth is, that script came out of what we do. We pitch, present ideas to clients and they blow it out or change it for the worse. Basically, we put our jobs on screen. ***Richard: With the Orange ads, did you have one celebrity in mind initially and then expand?*** Luke: We shot four at a time. And for that we had less money than for one Orange television campaign. Yan: It was very difficult. We would write dummy scripts but getting an actual celebrity was very hard and we didn't have a lot of money. If you got someone who was kind of interested they would ask 'what does my script look like.' So you would have to write a specific script for, for example,

Right
Luke's book
Pages from Luke's sketchbook

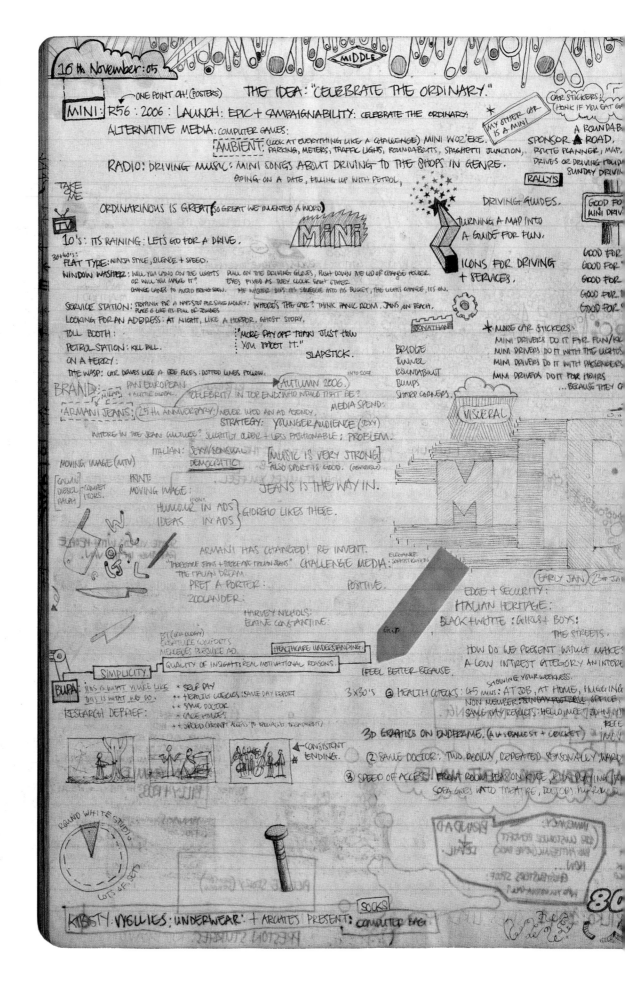

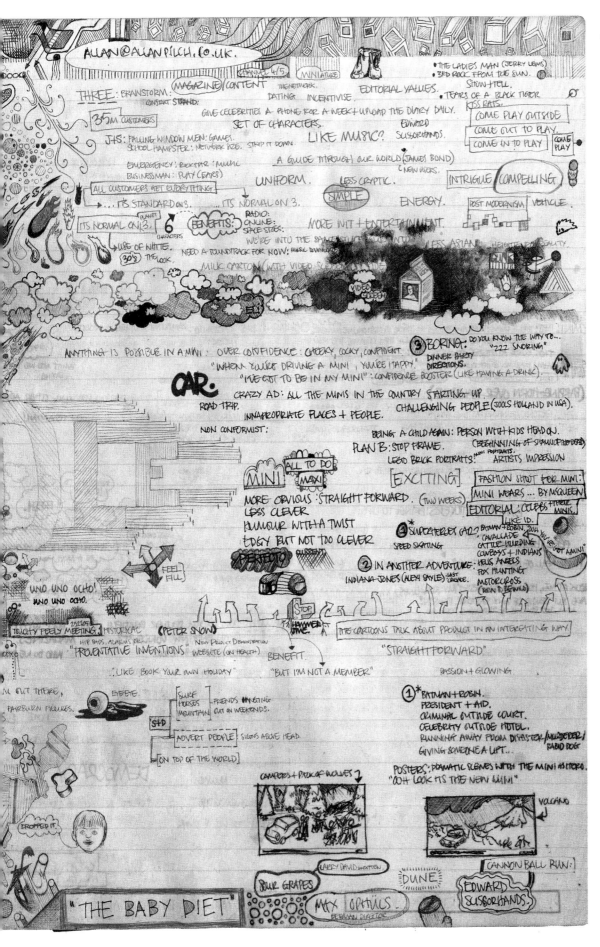

'We go out a lot and sit in coffee shops and talk. We go through a hell of a lot of thinking and discussing and usually the ideas come in the down-time, after you filter out all the crap'

This spread
Orange Cinema campaign
Featuring Patrick Swayze; Carrie
Fisher; Sean Astin; Spike Lee

Far right
Luke's book (detail)

Tim Robbins or whoever. And for every one celebrity
we got we ended up writing hundreds of scripts. Luke:
So we would be shooting in two days' time without
any celebrity booked. So you are on the phone all
the fucking time, to agents who might say 'I've got
this person interested,' and then you write scripts for
them, etc. etc. Very difficult.

***Richard: Did the celebrities say yes because they
liked what you do, the script? Or was it for the
money?*** Luke: The first round was very difficult
because we hadn't made any so no one had a reference
point. The only reason we got who we got was because
of Alan Cumming, who weirdly enough we'd met a few
times in Los Angeles, but he didn't really know us.
But he took the job, he said because as a Scotsman
he understood the comedy, he knew Orange and…
'OK, £40,000. I'll do it.' He's massive in America and
because he said he was onboard everyone else said
'I'll do it'. Yan: Spike Lee said, 'I hear you've got Alan
Cumming, I'll do it'. Luke: Then Carrie Fisher said
she'd do it. Then finally Roy Scheider. Yan: When we
got Patrick Swayze he had Dirty Dancing II coming
out, so it was good timing for him. Luke: Also, he loves
comedy. He was awesome, he was so up for doing
stuff. 'I'll play it up how you want to play it up. I'll
play it down.' He was so up for doing his spot. Yan:
We had a really great cast. We also had a really great
crew who were really into the job and we kept using
the same crew for two or three years. Always efficient
and professional and they'd have a cigarette at the
back and say, 'it's always a great pleasure to do these
spots, they're really funny'. ***Richard: Did you know
from the beginning the ads were going to work?***
Luke: We had a feeling that it was a good idea. Even
before production. And then when you're doing comedy
you're ad-libbing as you are going. Then you yell
'cut' and the whole crew is laughing. Then you know
you've got something pretty good. Yan: We over-wrote
the scripts. The key is, we got a good cast to be the
Orange film board and they do spark off one another
and give you gems. They know the idea, then they ad-
lib, continually adjusting to fit into sixty seconds. We
had to have a tight version.

*'When you're doing
comedy you're ad-
libbing as you are
going. Then you yell
'cut' and the whole
crew is laughing. Then
you know you've got
something pretty good'*

Richard: What was your favourite ad in the series?
Yan: Verne Troy. Luke: Steven Seagal [not yet
released] because of all the explosions and special
effects. But he was difficult – he showed up with

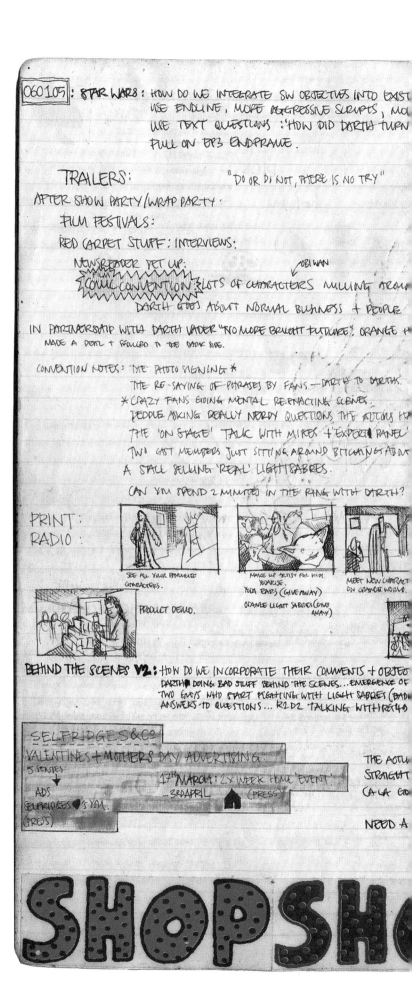

'I think there is the suspicion that you're trying to do one over someone. This leaves me baffled. Why would I want to make a bad ad for you?'

bodyguards. I found the most talented people are the easiest, the least talented cause the most fuss. Roy Scheider turned up on set, read the script twice, did his whole day. Really helpful. Really polite. Drove himself to the set, then drove himself back to the Hamptons, and lay in the road for two days in a war protest. Such a dude. **Richard: I had a similar experience with the actor Laurence Fishburne. He agreed to narrate a documentary on Muhammad Ali. He shows up at the studio. Reads a forty-five minute script without having to repeat one sentence. There is a reason why they are who they are.** Yan: Exactly. When you saw Roy Scheider do it, it was almost as if we didn't write it any more. He owned it. He's talking to the crew before you yell 'action.' You yell 'action' and he's in the zone. Luke: We looked at each other and thought 'fucking hell, this is going to be good!'

Richard: Do you want to go into film or television? Luke: Something longer-format is always appealing, a sitcom or a book. I don't know what I would do if an opportunity came along. What would be nice would be to take the client out of the picture and write about a pure idea, a proper story. We have ideas now but we haven't really got the time. It would be great to do a sitcom but it's finding the time. Yan: We should make the time. **Richard: How often do you say, 'I don't want to do this ad'?** Yan: You don't get that choice, unless you run your own agency. **Richard: After the Orange ad, I assume that takes you to a higher place.** Yan: Yes, it does. And that's one of the reasons why we are creative directors instead of creative team. Luke: Whether that holds any sway with clients, we've yet to see… Yan: It's all based on trust. If you have done a good job for a client, as you do the next jobs it becomes easier. It's hard coming to a new agency. The client doesn't know us from Adam. So we have to prove ourselves with the new clients. It's hard. Luke: Sometimes clients seem to think that you are doing things purely for your creative ego… Yan: Which is not the way we think at all. We realize there is a business problem here that needs solving. We need, in marketing terms, to position ourselves somewhere

different to other people. Luke: I think there is the suspicion, it's quite old school, that you're trying to do one over someone. Mother had some clients like that. This leaves me baffled. Why would I want to make a bad ad for you? Yan: Why would we shoot ourselves in the foot? So you take the business elsewhere! Luke: It takes two to tango. Good creative work only exists because good clients have the vision to buy and invest in it. Yan: Or they understand that perhaps they don't know the best way to do creative work and they leave it to the agency. The best clients are the ones that say, 'I trust you to do that, I'll just make sure it's on strategy'. **Richard: Are your clients sometimes like accountants?** Yan: They can be. Sometimes there's a lot of money on the line and they have to defend their decisions to someone above them. **Richard: Is it true to say that advertising in England tends to be wittier and more progressive than in the States?** Luke: In general, yes. But I still think some of the best ads come out of America.

Richard: When you argue and fall out, who makes up first? Yan: We don't argue. Luke. Yes we do. Yan: The only times we argue is when we're down about the industry. When we have been knocked a few times. Luke: Or when our work has been blown out by a client, which is frustrating. **Richard: Do you buy each other birthday and Christmas presents?** Luke: One of us does. Yan: I owe him. **Richard: What did you get him?** Luke: A vintage Honda Tamiya model kit from eBay. 1960s, I think. We like toys, but really odd rare toys. Basically, I buy them for myself, feel bad and then give them to him. Yan: Meanwhile, I bought him nothing for Christmas and he's got his birthday coming up. Luke: You can do a double.

Richard: Your ads have wit. Does that mean you're depressives? Yan: No. I think we're both very up, positive people. Luke: A lot of people in the world take themselves very seriously. They think that advertising is very, very important. There are lots of columns, lots of editorial about it. A lot of letter-writing. Basically, it's just a fucking ad break. Thirty seconds in-between a body of work that is really interesting.

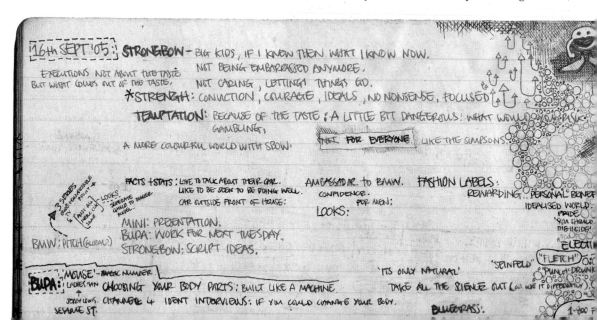

It's not rocket science. We don't take it seriously, as in national politics… Yan: Viewers aren't interested in ad breaks. You've got to cut through and entertain them in thirty seconds. People like a laugh. I think we are in the entertainment industry. 'I like that. I'd like to see that again, please.' Luke: Clients sometimes forget about the consumer. 'We want to say this, this and this.' What's in it for the viewer engaging with it? Nothing. Yan: You don't want someone to introduce something to you and just shout at you about whatever they want to talk about. Luke: Yeah, like 'let's talk about me.' Yan: I think that's also why we do a lot of humour. If you get a reaction from someone, if they laugh, you've won them over. Luke: Also if you talk about the truth, and they can recognize the truth, they will respect you that little bit more.

Richard: What is your Kryptonite? Luke: It's got to be departmental politics. Not fucking interested, don't fucking care. My only objective is solving the problem and getting good work out. And there is so much departmental politics, client side, agency side, and there probably always will be but it is so dull. Yan: People who find reasons not to do stuff. *Richard: I think that's it. I think you've told me all I need. Thank you.*

Later, I thought about what Yan and Luke said, about always looking for the truth of the product, the truth of the brand, and I decided maybe H.G. Wells believed advertising is legalized lying, but maybe he was just having a bad day. I think I was wrong to describe Yan and Luke's house style as wit – it's more entertainment, humour. And as E.B. White once said, analysing humour is like dissecting a frog. Few people are interested and the frog dies of it. So I won't bother.

* * *

Above
Orange Cinema campaign
Featuring Verne Troy

Left
Luke's book (detail)

Zip Design is a London-based graphic design consultancy established in 1996 by Peter Chadwick. As a seven-strong team, our main objective is to progress and celebrate mainstream image-making through intelligent design. Print campaigns, including band and label identity for the music industry, have kept Zip continually busy, but the company has proved itself equally fluent in other areas. In recent years clients have diversified, and the projects we now undertake have widened to embrace branding, websites, e-flyers, motion graphics, books, brochures, typefaces, even TV titles. Alongside these key cultural disciplines Zip also handles all manner of art direction, bringing our unique sensibilty to clients as disparate as Paul Smith and MTV. Whatever the project, we strive to apply soul, unbridled energy and a meticulous sense of detail to everything we undertake.

info@zipdesign.co.uk
www.zipdesign.co.uk

How does your story begin? In a galaxy far, far, away. *What was your favourite story as a child?* Stig of the Dump. *What is the background to that story?* A kid falls in a pit of rubbish and finds Stig – a tramp-like character who can't speak English. *What was the twist in the plot?* If there was one, then I missed it … *How would you define your character?* Changeable. *Who is your hero or heroine?* Aslan the lion. *Who are you at war with?* Skeletor. *Who or what are you in love with?* My iPod. Materialistic, yes? *What is the character you most identify with?* Me? *If your life was turned into a Hollywood movie, who would you like to play your role?* A robot with special super animatronics. *What is the Holy Grail?* Something that Indiana Jones was looking for. *In what form do the aliens appear?* Sting. *Biblical stories: what are your ten commandments?* Never wear matching socks; eat lots of fruit; don't listen to idiots; don't make eye contact with people in the street; be polite and act with decorum; avoid inappropriate touching in the workplace; colour co-ordinate everything; utilise caffeine; hang tough; trust no one. *Special effects? Do you use any?* Smoke and mirrors. *What's your kryptonite?* Kryptonite. *Famous last line?* 'I told you I was ill.' (Spike Milligan)

references
ripts from the
ns that frame the
a paragraph or
self so in essence
ld without reading
o the sentence used
he actual story – it

w the earth began
vegetation and
global warming
dle and end. Past,

00

01

02

03

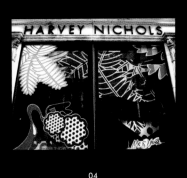

04

05

06

07

08

Atypyk

Atypyk is not a boy band
Atypyk sounds Greek, but is actually French
Atypyk is full of spelling mistakes
Atypyk is a friendly business
Atypyk has no marketing department
Atypyk enjoys making completely unnecessary things
Atypyk is much younger than you are
Atypyk thinks that humans are wonderful (sometimes)
Atypyk will always tell nothing but the truth
Atypyk products contains small parts, dangerous for children
Atypyk kills flies (sorry)
Atypyk does not have the key to success
Atypyk loves happy endings

contact@atypyk.com
www.atypyk.com

How does your story begin? Well. *What was your favourite story as a child?* The ones I created while playing. *What is the background to that story?* To bring all those famous characters for children out of their world. *What was the twist in the plot?* No plot. But many twists. *How would you define your character?* Oh, pleeease. *Who are the bad guys?* Not me. *Who are the good guys?* Not me. *Who are you at war with?* Myself. *Who or what are you in love with?* Siren, my girlfriend. *What is the character you most identify with?* The Invisible Man. *If your life was turned into a Hollywood movie, who would you like to play your role?* I would prefer to have that as a surprise. *What is the holy grail?* It is said that it was a cup or a plate. *Is your life an Odyssey or an Iliad?* Most of all, a mess. *In what form do the aliens appear?* Human. Definitely. *Biblical stories: what are your ten commandments?* I only have one: Thou shalt not accept any commandment. *Special effects? Do you use any?* A few. *What's your kryptonite?* Long walks in the city. *Who's your ideal audience?* Any human beings. *What's a happy ending?* When people are happy…? *Famous last line:* 'The end.'

Sweet World
2005
A collection of PEZ candy dispensers, hand transformed by Atypyk. Several times a year, PEZ launches a new collection of world-famous characters (from TV series, cartoons, games, superheroes, events, fairy tales, films, etc). They have been doing this for more than fifty years; thousands of different characters have been produced. Atypyk has transformed those fictitious characters into characters that are much more of a down-to-earth reality.

00a

00b

01

02

03

04

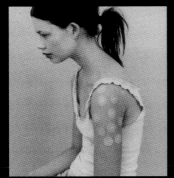

05

06

07

00a
Ivan

00b
Jean-Sebastian

01
Betough
Wear a gun.

02
Cklein
Nappies for babies.

03
Cowstick
Get a cow in your kitchen.
6 Self-adhesive cow patches.

04
Mic
Sing in the shooOOOower.

05
Patch
For the treatment of addiction to love.

06
Plaster
Sticking plaster diamond ring.

07
Play with guns
Recycling of guns into a skipping rope.

MR BEAN (DESERVED) BLACK EYE

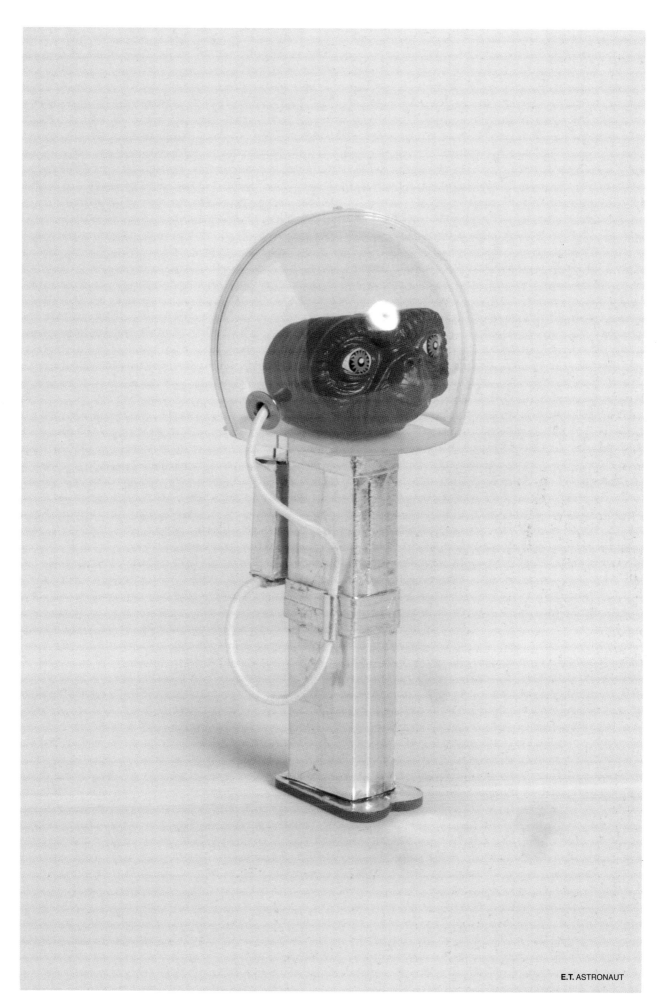

E.T. ASTRONAUT

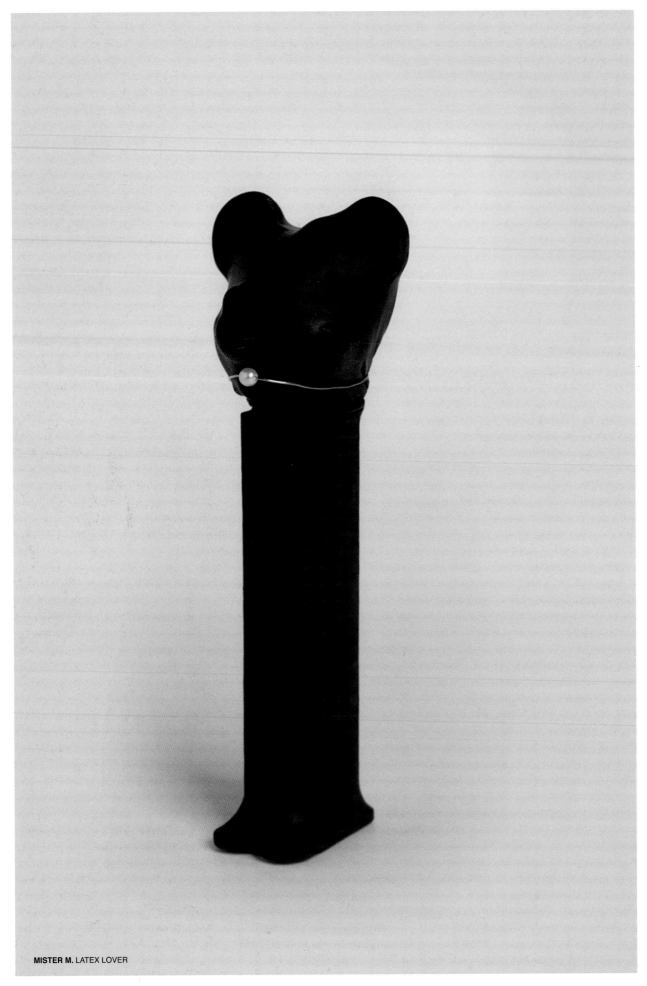

MISTER M. LATEX LOVER

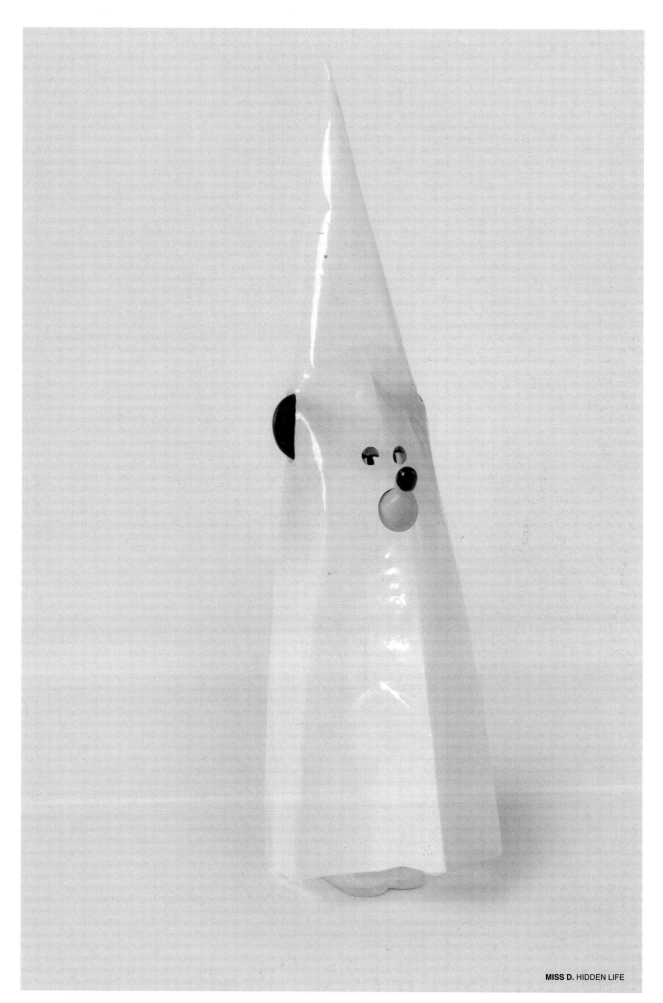

MICKEY HAPPY BELIEVER

Barnstormers

A conversation with David Ellis

Is the barn really for real? Yes, it was originally built in the mid-20th century to cure tobacco. *Did you really move it?* Yes, twice. We borrowed it for the 2004 show at the South Eastern Center for Contemporary Art (SECCA) in Winston Salem, North Carolina, about two hours drive from Cameron where the barn was originally built. It took three days to take down and three days to rebuild each time. Mike Houston, the mastermind behind this project, engineered the task, which required a sensitive hammer. She was a delicate old lady.

Why? Everyone in this crew has a special love for exterior painting. The main idea was to bring a little of that exterior world inside. It could have been anything, but in North Carolina we have a lot of tobacco barns. It's just a normal everyday focal point that spatters the landscape. I painted on these very same barns, starting at age twelve. I wrote words with letters taller than me and that spelled out monikers like 'shock', 'Assoc' and 'skwerm'. I saw immediately that I was reaching people driving by on the road. That was my spark to make art my life. It seemed to me that even on that tiny, winding state road the passers-by represented a bigger slice of the American pie than those who would ever go to a gallery or museum. Knowing that everyday someone driving by in a truck would become an unsuspecting viewer of my art gave me a reason for being. The idea of simply hanging paintings on the wall of a museum doesn't inspire me in the same way. The idea of making art with the intent of selling it doesn't motivate me. The idea of bringing a barn into a museum and painting on it dozens of times with my favourite artists in the world and returning it to a farm where it is immediately covered with tar paper and filled with hay bales gets me up in the morning, fully charged.

Was there a precise criteria behind the choice of collaborators? The best artists I've met in New York. People whose work forces me to dig deeper in my own shed. *Are they people you often work with?* They are my friends, people I respect highly and work with as often as possible, though it is becoming more rare these days as we are slammed on our individual pursuits. This project brought together some greats: Chuck Webster, Martin Mazorra, Sasu, Kami, Madsaki, Che Jen, José Parla, Chris Mendoza, Mike Houston, Alex Lebedev, Mike Ming, Swoon, Daikon, South, Kiku Yamaguchi, David Ellis, Maya Hayuk, Blust One, West One, Yuri Shimojo, Kenji Hirata, and Rostarr. *How do you feel your styles interact?* Like a conversation. Someone lays down a form, someone answers that form with another form. On it goes like this, the forms evolve, eventually something new is born. *Do they ever clash?* Almost always there's some kind of tension. It usually makes us all paint better, work harder, think deeper. *Was the barn being painted over and over again?* Yes, many, many times over. No special effects, all live. *Over what period of time?* Three months.

What came out of the repainting? A narrative, an idea? Each new layer addresses the whole like an avalanche, equal parts build and destroy. *I know you show a lot in art galleries. Do you consider yourself as part of the 'art world' or of another scene?* In my mind, art is not something easily contained within quotes or scenes or frames or walls or halls or film or time… It is a force that begins and ends, where we do not know. *Do you ever sell the barns?* The barns are in use. They are one hundred percent NFS.

Coasthomson

Coasthomson: Visual intelligence to build Brands.
Founded in 2005 by Christopher Thomson, Mark Thomson and Frédéric Vanhorenbeke. Coasthomson have offices in London & Brussels.

www.coasthomson.com

How does your story begin? [Frédéric/Mark/Christopher] By accident/In the future/1969. *What was your favourite story as a child?* Captain America/*Fantastic Mr Fox*/Richard Scarry. *How would you define your character?* Multiple/Cunning/Naughty. *What is the character you most identify with?* Elvis/Best supporting actor/Naughty. *If your life was turned into a Hollywood movie, who would you like to play your role?* Jim Carrey/Robert de Niro in Taxi Driver/Monica Bellucci. *Ghost stories: what haunts you?* Graduation Day/Did I leave the iron on?/Waste. *Horror stories: what really scares you?* Darkness/Cold porridge/Me. *Spy movies: has anyone ever ripped you off or spied on your work and stole professional secrets from you?* Yes/There are no secrets with me/Shhh. *Do you spy on other people's work? Who do you spy on?* I spy on everybody/If I told you I'd have to kill you/The neighbours. *Special effects? Do you use any?* Ubiquity/Smoke and mirrors/Alcohol. *What's a happy ending?* That's all folks/It's goodnight from me and it's goodnight from him/I love you. *Famous last line:* First line ... Sometimes you wake up dead, there's a gun in your hand and its pointing at your head/The End/I am just going outside and may be sometime.

Narrative: 'Fire'
Gripping, moving, epic. A narrative broken down to basic, symbolic elements. Timeless, universal, primaeval. A story of life and death beginnings and endings.

Photography by Colin Hawkins, represented by: www.untitled.co.uk

00

01

02

03

04

05

06

07

08

00
Mark Thomson (UK)
Christopher Thomson (UK)
Frédéric Vanhorenbeke (B)

01
Preen
Invitation

02
Centre de Chant Choral
Identity

03
Culture Club Volume 4
CD packaging

04
Millennium
Book design

05
Gerd: Fire in My Soul
12" record sleeve art direction and design

06
ICA
I see music exhibition
catalogue design

07, 08
Major Players
Identity system

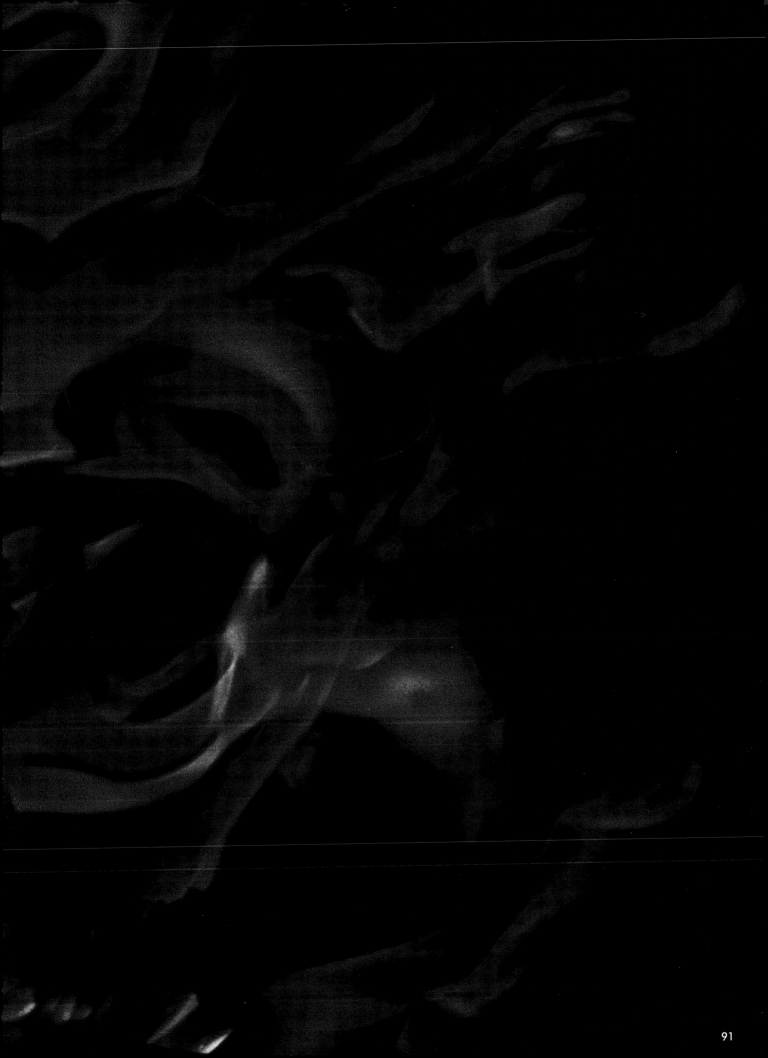

FRANCIS ROVE®–DARK BUSINESS is published by Stop-ill Publishing. Created by Dennis Eriksson. Office of Publication. Skeppsbron 10, 111 30 Stockholm, Sweden. Copyright © 2006 Dennis Eriksson/Stop-ill. All rights reserved. Contact: info@stop-ill.com. Other episodes is to be found at: www. stop-ill.com/francisrove. All characters, their destinctive likenesses and related indicia featured in this publication are trademarks of Dennis Eriksson/Stop-ill. The stories, characters and incidents featured in this publication are entirely fictional.

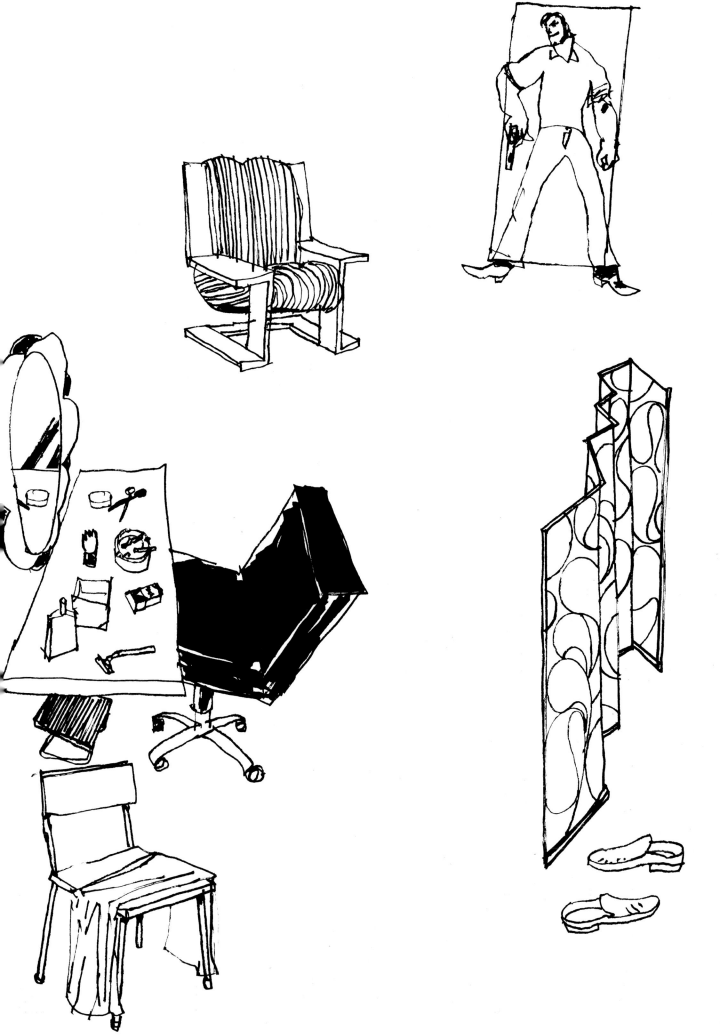

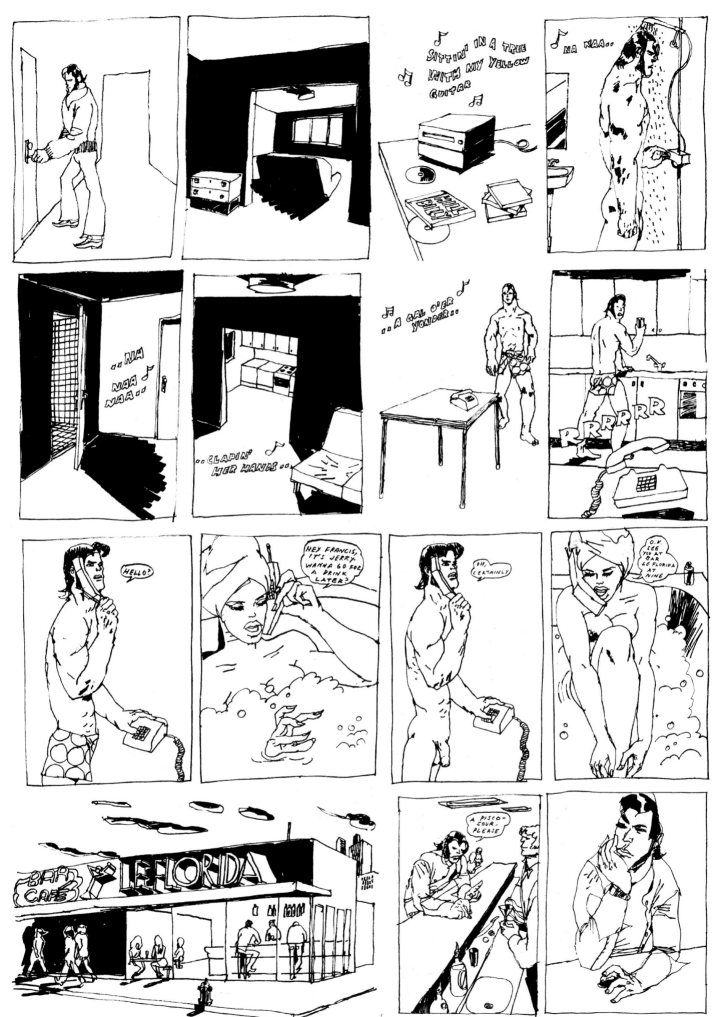

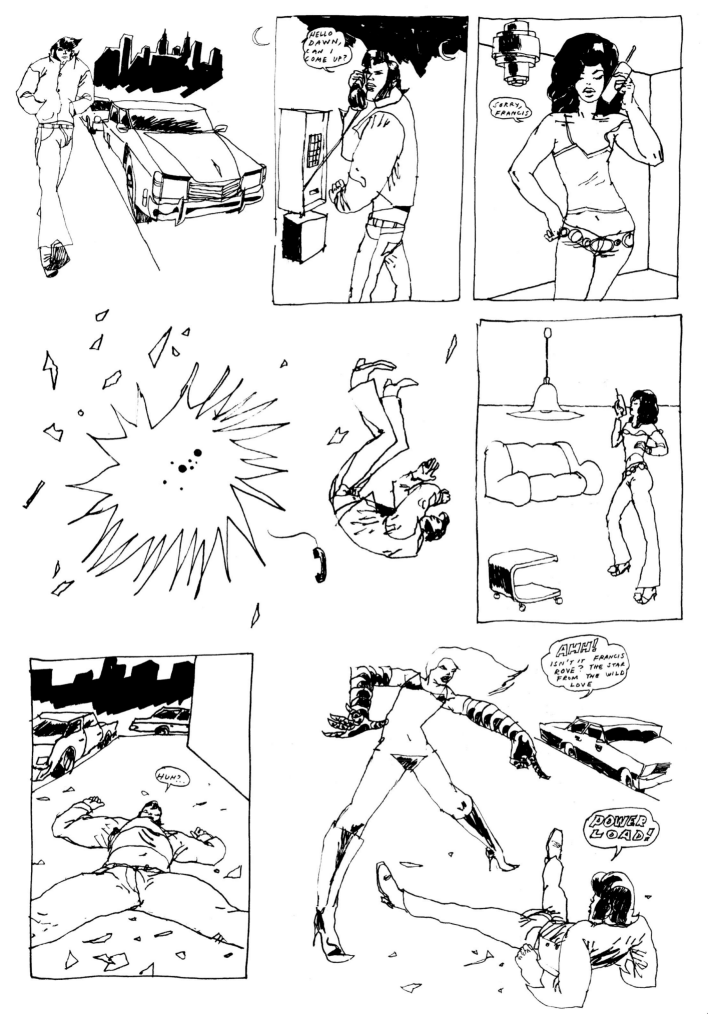

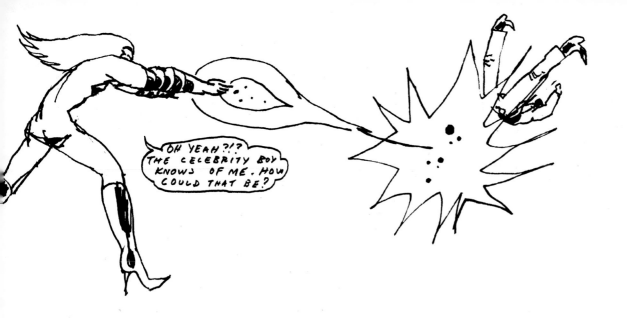

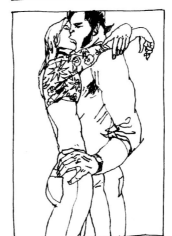

...usiness
...isode in long series
..., a non-married
...rly thirties, who
...rough. He lives a
...Cobalter. The plot
...d his co-actors and
...Florinda Flames,
...n love with. A lot
...speedos, burger-
...nudity, drama,
...ng the visuals of
...mple and rough
...details. When it's
...f violent way with
...g of motion. I never
...k pen, scotch tape,
...ncil makes me
...the drawing.

Dennis Eriksson graduated in 1997 after four years of art studies at the Konstfack University College of Arts Craft and Design in Stockholm, and one year at the Rhode Island School of Design in Providence, RI (USA). Since then he has worked as a freelance illustrator for both Swedish and international clients. Dennis Eriksson's style can be described as lively and full of movement, with straggling lines and strong colours. His inspiration comes from *Krazy Kat* and *John Carter, Warlord of Mars*, American soap operas from the 70s, and Raymond Pettibon record covers. His work include book covers, animated videos and commercials, posters, ad campaigns and editorial illustration. In 2004 he launched his comic book *Francis Rove*.
His clients include Atlas Förlag, Goodyear, *NK Stil* magazine, *RES* magazine, Halebop, The Hellacopters, *Dagens Nyheter* newspaper, Luger, *BLM* magazine, the COOP supermarket chain, *After Hours* magazine, *Big* magazine, and *Jane* magazine.

How does your story begin? It begins with Francis Rove shooting a scene with his co-actress Florinda Flames. She's wearing tight pants, he's wearing loafers. *Who is your hero or heroine?* My grandad was a hero of mine. He passed away two years ago at the age of 94. He liked chewing tobacco, liquor and listening to the radio. *What is the character you most identify with?* I'm named after Dennis the Menace so I would have to say him. *Biblical stories: what are your ten commandments?* Do not play computer games; do not tattoo and pierce; do not wear leather; learn to eat ALL kinds of food; listen to your gut feeling; do not eat hot dogs in the subway or on the bus; respect old people; kick spoiled brats' asses; do not live where you grew up; invent. *Spy movies: has anyone ever ripped you off or spied on your work and stole professional secrets from you?* When I started working eight years ago there were clients who didn't wanna pay. I remember an agency who only paid me 1,000 euros instead of the 4,000 I wanted. But afterwards they were very eager to have me over for a sauna session. A weird thing to offer a guy you just ripped off. *What's a happy ending?* Incognito with a highball drink by the pool, in the shade, in a foreign country. *Famous last line:* Hej hopp i lingonskogen! (Tally-ho in the Lingonberry forest!).

00

01

02

03

04

05

06

07

08

02
After Hours
I was commissioned to do front and back cover to the Japanese music magazine *After Hours*. The back illustration had the same hand lettering but another image. Actually, this is the back cover. The Japanese read from back to front.

03
Dad's swim-pants
Cover illustration about men's swimwear for ...Stan

04
Gal with Green Bikini and Glasses
This one is for Swedish fashion Magazine *NK Stil*. They wanted nice girls in comfy velour tracksuits and bikinis. A fun commission. I like drawing nice girls.

05
Ghost
An editorial illustration for *Dagen Nyheter*, a big Swedish morning newspaper

06
Jerry Nouveau
Self commission

07
Orchestra
An editorial illustration for *Dagens Nyheter*.

08
Taxi
A cover piece for *PåStan, Dagens Nyheter's* weekend special

I pursued studies in illustration and animated film in Brussels during which I directed two short movies. I was later chosen as animator for the cartoon film *Les Triplettes de Belleville* by Sylvain Chomet. While I was working on this film, I started collecting objects, all sorts of things for no apparent reason, although I was already creating small figurative characters. Little by little my assembly took more and more importance and of all the materials I was collecting, plastic naturally imposed itself. Finally my collaboration with the photographer Bernard Babette enriched the visual aspect of my work and helped me widen my narrative research. My work is promoted by Costume3pièces.

www.costume3pieces.com

How does your story begin? All of sudden. *What was your favourite story as a child?* Treasure Island. *Who are the bad guys?* The hole in the ozone layer. *Who are the good guys?* Penguins. *Who is your hero or heroine?* Plastic Bertrand. *Who are you at war with?* With my shoes that squeak all the time. *Who or what are you in love with?* A photo by Martin Parr. *If your life was turned into a Hollywood movie, who would you like to play your role?* Animal from the *Muppet Show*. *Is your life an Odyssey or an Iliad?* I don't like travel. *In what form do the aliens appear?* Pistachio ice cream. *Biblical stories: what are your ten commandments?* Recycle; recycle; recycle; recycle, etc … *Ghost stories: what haunts you?* That my characters throw me out of a window. *Horror stories: what really scares you?* Big dogs that drool. *Special effects? Do you use any?* Only Bernard Babette. *What's your kryptonite?* Supermarkets. *Who's your ideal audience?* A hysterical female audience. *What's a happy ending?* When the rabbit goes to eat his chips with hunter's sauce (hunter's sauce is a Belgian speciality). *Famous last line:* Thanks to all the members of the Recycle Club.

Ba; Biba; Dark Vador; Ice Penguin; Maternité; Guide protecteur
Photography: Bernard Babette

My work is based on collecting, gathering; objects or parts of objects mainly made of plastic found on pavements, in bins of flea markets or brought by friends and family, members of the Recycle Club. I then commit to a simple principle as I assemble; that is, original colours and shapes of the collected parts may not be modified. New plastic figurative and non-figurative objects are created and given a new environment … a second life, which Bernard Babette then captures with his camera.

00

01

02

03

04

05

06

07

08

00
Olivier Goka

01
Mon atelier

02
La famille Babette
Photography: Bernard Babette

03
Nintendo Space car
'Création original pour le lancement de la console *Game Boy Advance SP Pink* édition aux salon du prêt à porter Paris 2004 et exposition chez Colette Paris.'

04
Pic-vert
Photography: Bernard Babette

05–08
Baby robots
'Exhibition *les déchets contre attaquent*, Galerie 1sur1, Bruxelles 2004.'
Photography: Bernard Babette

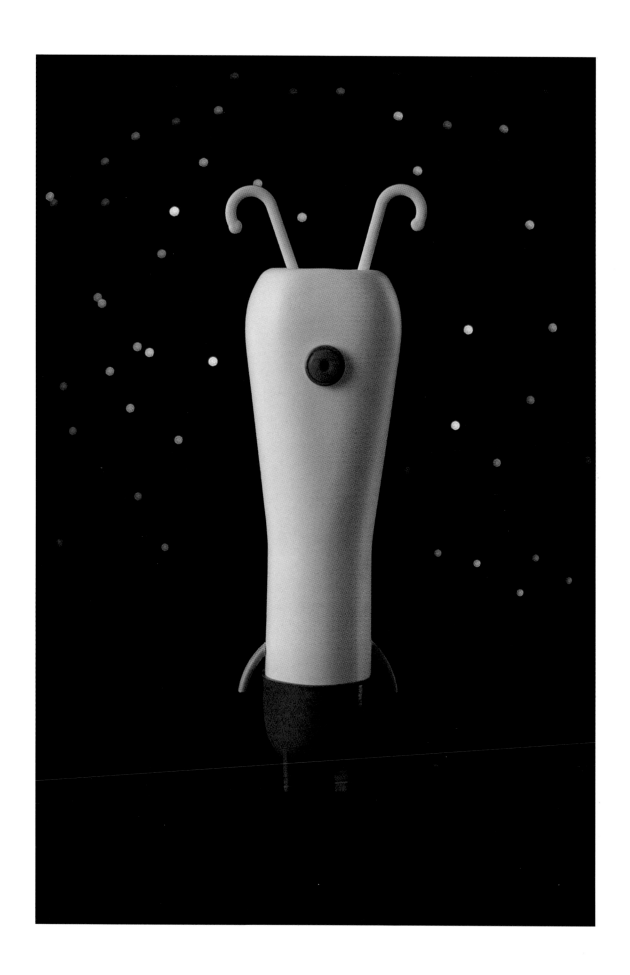

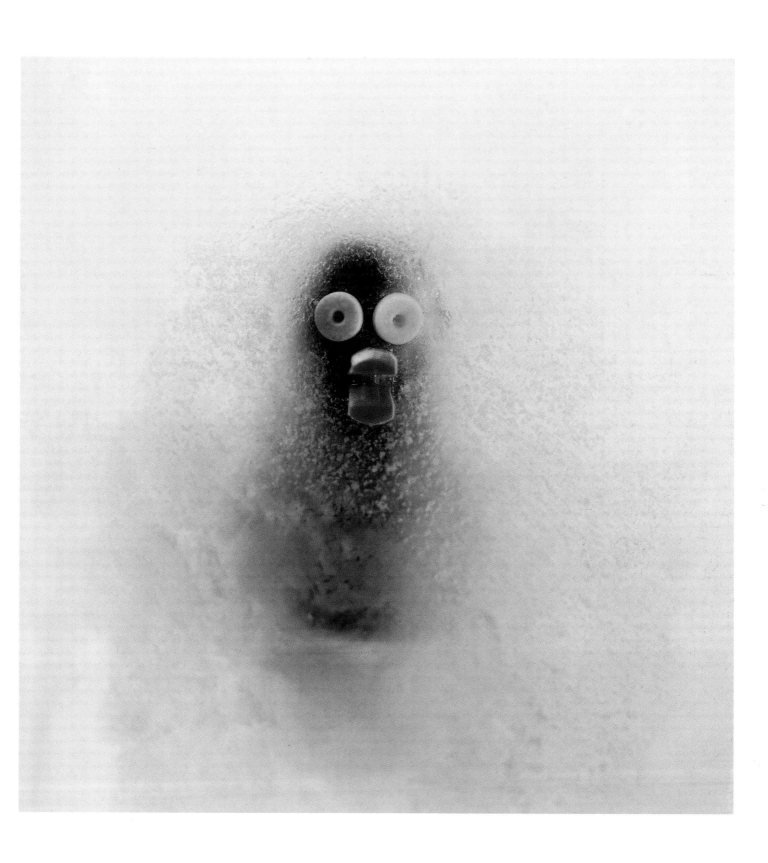

Sayo Iara Inomata

Dream
06.02.2006

It's the story of my dream, but actually it's not a story. There's no storyline or conclusion, no hero or villain. I think all dreams are rarely stories. In my dream there are many adjacent images and that's how it becomes one dream. When I'm dreaming, I feel there's someone projecting his / her view onto the screen in my mind. Perhaps the dream is just reflecting my desires but I think it's not only about that, so I start to think there's someone working in the dream cinema and trying to entertain me while I'm asleep. This time my dream monster showed me an upside-down world: the bat girls are living in the boxed toilet and when you go inside, there's another world, the world of freaks. The freaks entertain me and the show must go on, till I wake up.

Born on 16th September 1982. Japanese / Brazilian. Living in London, also sometimes in the dream world. Graduated Kingston-upon-Thames University, illustration / animation BA. Currently studying at the Royal College of Art, printed textile course, but from this year actually I'm talking a year out to find scholarship and sponsors to go back to the college. At the moment, I'm working for competitions, and hunting for a job. I'm almost becoming an expert at my mum's special chicken dish. Love drawing, music, underground films, good animation films, cool comic books, and a clean bathroom. Recently I'm starting to feel that I want to go back to Japan for the hot springs … it's all because of this weather. I love one hot spring which is at the top of a mountain; it's an amazing view because all you can see is only the sea and sky.

aquakingdom@hotmail.com

How does your story begin? When you fall asleep. *What was your favourite story as a child?* Peter Pan. *What is the background to that story?* It's all in the dream. *What was the twist in the plot?* Well, this story has no story. It just keeps going and growing. It's all happening in my dream world. *How would you define your character?* Freaks? *Who are the bad guys?* No bad guys. *Who are the good guys?* No good guys, either. *Who is your hero or heroine?* Slingsby Sandwich. *Who are you at war with?* Dad. *Who or what are you in love with?* Panini. *What is the character you most identify with?* Wednesday. *If your life was turned into a hollywood movie, who would you like to play your role?* Winona. *What is the holy grail?* Contact lenses. *Is your life an Odyssey or an Iliad?* Odyssey. *In what form do the aliens appear?* Boiled green pea. *Ghost stories: what haunts you?* Cat! *Horror stories: what really scares you?* Cat!! *Special effects: Do you use any?* Like *Star Wars? What's your kryptonite?* People in the streets. *Who's your ideal audience?* People who had a dream last night. *What's a happy ending?* When it ends the way I wanted it to be. *Famous last line:* The end.

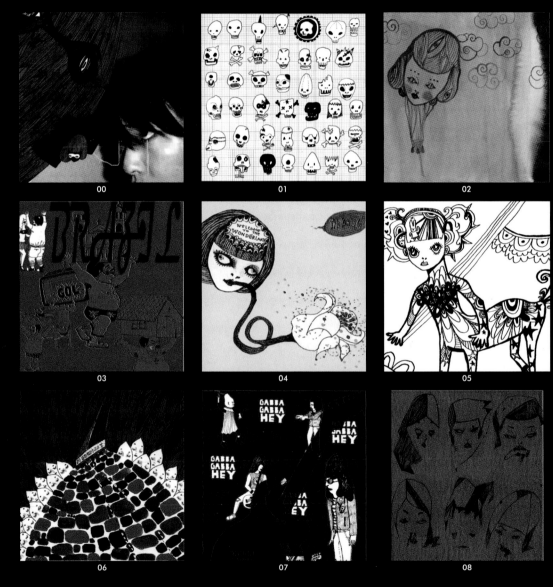

00
Sayo Iara Inomata

01
Skulls party
Pen drawing

02
Balloon head
Watercolour

03
Brazil
Pen drawing, Photoshop

04
Lily drag
Pen drawing, colour pencil

05
Pegasus
Pen drawing

06
Piccadilly
Watercolour, pen drawing

07
Ramonia
Pen drawing, Photoshop

08
Zombies
Screenprint on fabric

Dean Landry

Dean Landry (aka CHOOCH) is a self taught artist who hails from Harlem, NYC. His clients include Anna Sui, Cosmopolitan Magazine, The Strokes, and Nickelodeon to list a few. In 2003, Landry's *tromp l'oeil* designs were featured in two major art museum exhibitions. His Anna Sui illustrations can be seen in the book *Fashion & Graphics* published by Harper Design International. Landry's illustration artworks have also been used in major and independent movie releases. In addition to his work as a commercial artist, Landry is a painter, photographer, and musician. His vibrant paintings have been exhibited in the US and internationally. His photographs include a large body of Polaroid work, which spans the spectrum from beautiful to the grotesque.
His paintings, Polaroids and illustrations were featured in a solo show in Osaka, Japan in the summer of 2005. A small book of his illustrations and paintings was published to accompany this exhibit. He also performs and tours with his band, Johnny Cage Is A Fake.

choochland.com
johnnycageisafake.com

How does your story begin? He gets woken up by the sound of pigeons and rubs the sleep from his eyes. *What was your favourite story as a child?* David and Goliath. *How would you define your character?* He's an antisocial, fat, flinchy, never-comfortable kid who likes to draw pictures. *Who are the bad guys?* His imaginary enemies. *Who are the good guys?* His imaginary friends. *Who is your hero or heroine?* The loopy old man who doesn't care what anyone thinks. *Who are you at war with?* Myself. *Who or what are you in love with?* The people who lose / fail and come back to triumph. *What is the character you most identify with?* The loopy old man. *If your life was turned into a Hollywood movie, who would you like to play your role?* George 'The Animal' Steele or Godzilla. *What is the Holy Grail?* The perfect photo. *Is your life an Odyssey or an Iliad?* Iliad. *In what form do the aliens appear?* They look like harmless old ladies. *Ghost stories: what haunts you?* My childhood. *What's your kryptonite?* Food. *Who's your ideal audience?* People with eyes and ears. *What's a happy ending?* Taking a good picture. I can breath easy for the rest of the day. *Famous last line:* All I want is to make pictures and play my guitar.

Every Day
16.02.2006
When I was young, my parents bought me a Polaroid camera for Christmas. I was hooked immediately. I've always loved the instant gratification a Polaroid camera offers. I also like that each Polaroid picture is one of a kind and irreplaceable.
I try to take my cameras everywhere I go so I'm ready when a good photo presents itself. These photos were taken with an SX-70 and a Spectra Pro. They were taken between 2000–2006.

00

01

02

03

04

05

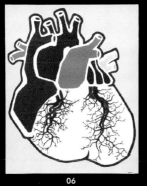
06

07

08

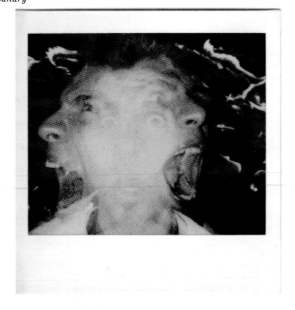

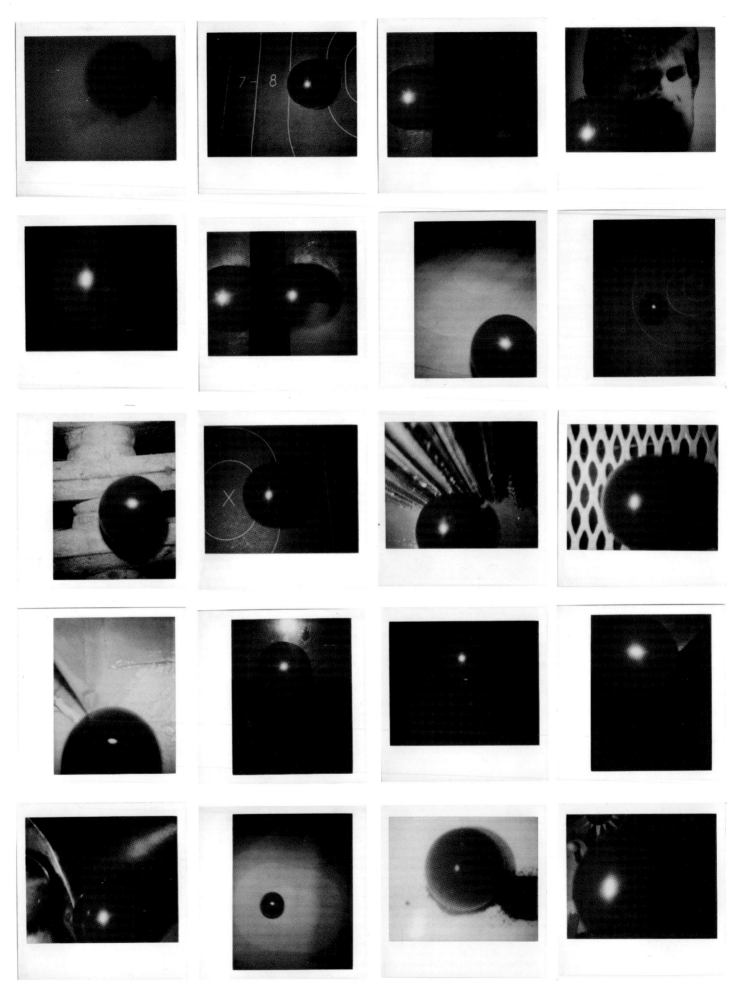

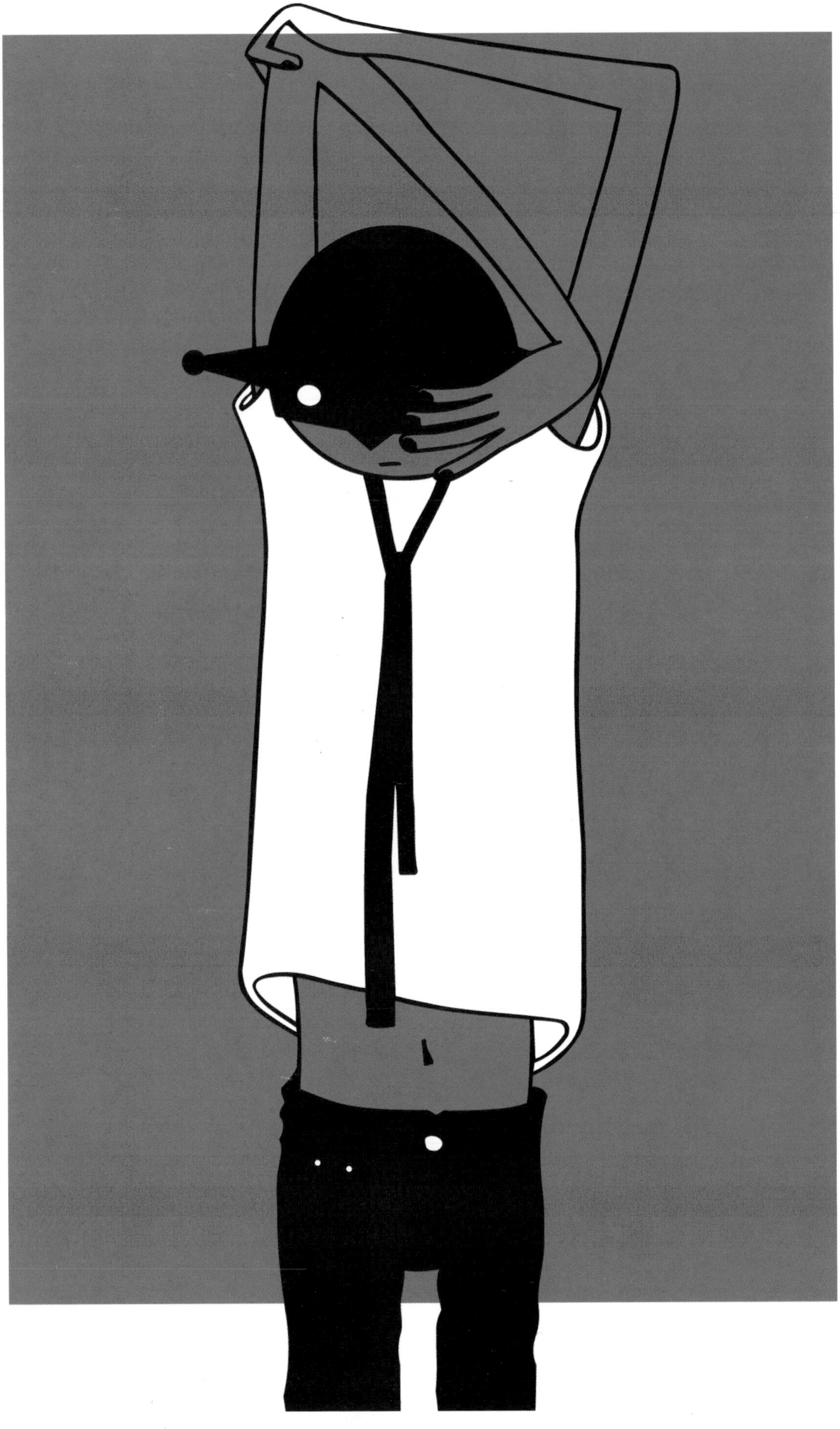

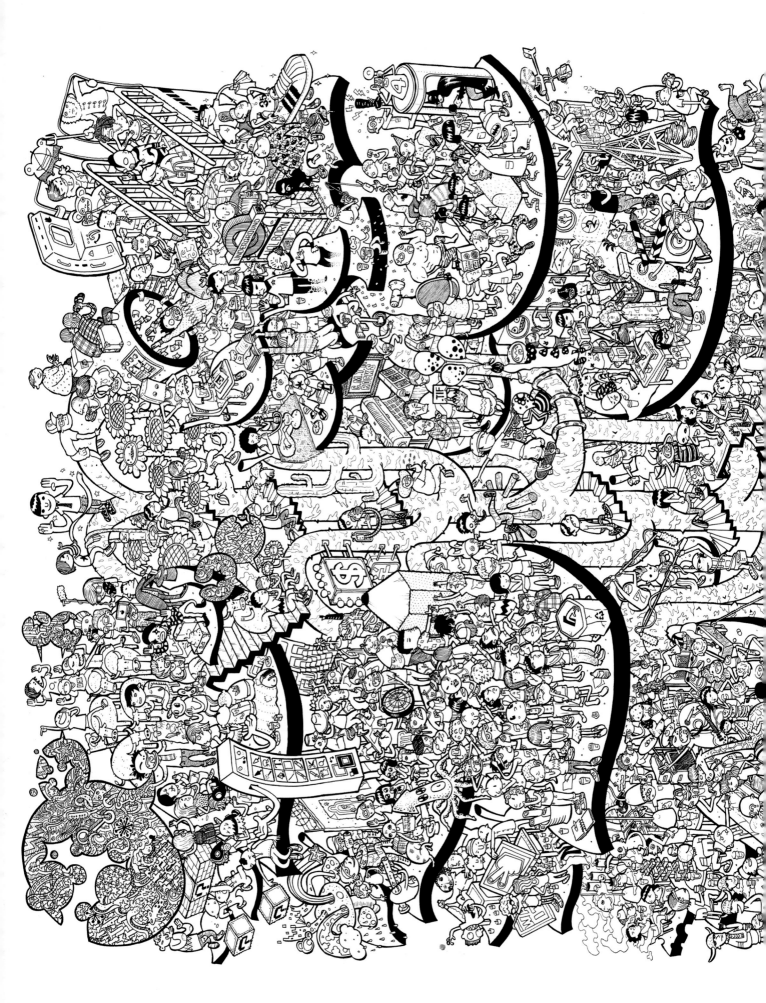

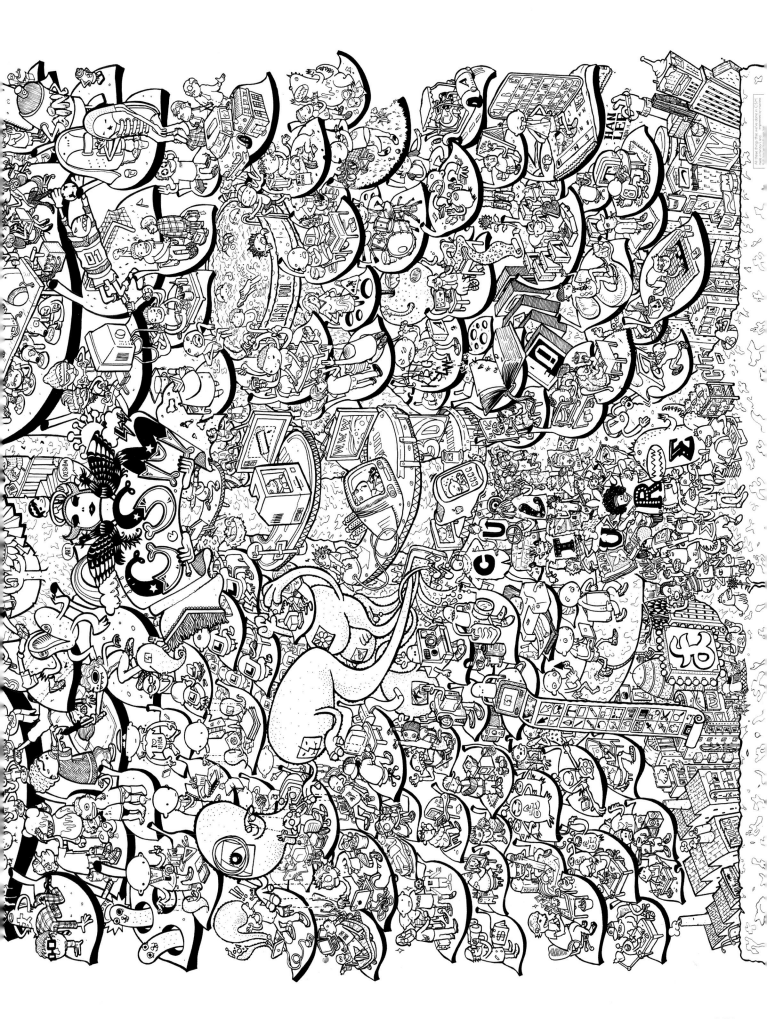

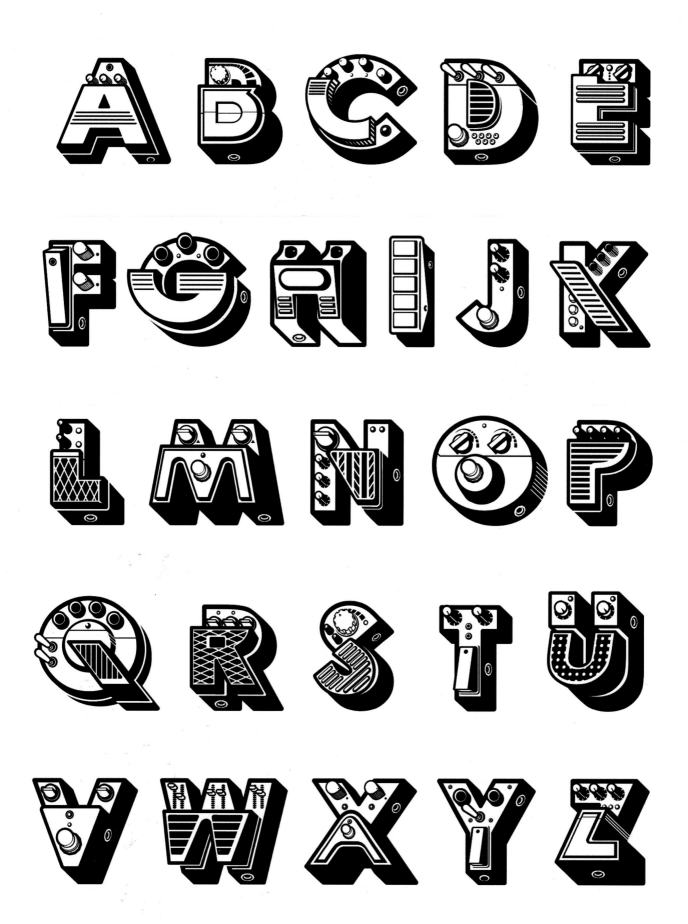

I enjoy creating characters the most, because to draw a character is not just to draw lines on paper, it needs some substance behind it. It could be a song, some food, a real person or a word…it does not need to be some big idea, but I am always think... lot when I draw them, and that makes me happ... like to make images that people can spend a lo... looking at the details of. Everyone likes a story to understand the characters, and that is what... to achieve. I like to tell a story in a poster, to... show a lot of information on one image, and you may get surprised when you see it from time to time.

How does your story begin? A Taiwanese boy who loves to draw. *What was your favourite story as a child?* Dragon Ball Z. *How would you define your character?* Homer Simpson – big belly + big mac ÷ 2 + Smurf hat × futureboi100 + ? = haniboi. *Who is your hero or heroine?* My Dad and Mum. *Who are you at war with?* A character like me is not allowed to fight in the story. *Who or what are you in love with?* Harumelon, TV and fast food. *What is the character you most identify with?* Han Solo. *If your life was turned into a Hollywood movie, who would you like to play your role?* I would like to play myself. Movie stars can make more money than illustrators. *In what form do the aliens appear?* American president, no doubt about it. *Spy movies: has anyone ever ripped you off or spied on your work and stole professional secrets from you? Do you spy on other people's work? Who do you spy on?* The window display in Nike Town two years ago, it was 90% like the window display I did for a shop on Carnaby Street. *What's your kryptonite?* T.V. I would not be able to walk if I face it. *Who's your ideal audience?* Rope-skipping bikini model. *What's a happy ending?* Typical cheesy Hollywood ending. *Famous last line:* Oops!

00

01

02

03

04

05

06

07

08

07
Future boy
The most recent character I have done. Everything about *Future boy* is the opposite of me.

08
Sketch of myself
A sketch I did before I went to college, surprisingly like I am now! Sketching is the most important part of my work, all the images I have done come from my sketchbooks.

...h book. This ... project, 99%

03
Work for Puma
A commercial work I did for Puma, I illustrated a few Puma shoes into characters.

04
Any rock'n'roll for me
A poster with 170 characters, each character is inspired by a rock song I like

...mputer, in this ...ustration into an A3 ... shop.

05
Logo for Any rock'n'roll for me
Any rock'n'roll for me is also the biggest band ever, and this is the logo for it.

06
Rock font
Font made from guitar effects pedals.

Less Rain

Less Rain is a digital design agency based in London and Berlin, founded in 1997 by Vassilios Alexiou and Lars Eberle. Over the last 10 years we have produced a variety of high quality, concept driven, tailor made solutions for an interactive environment across a range of digital platforms.

We offer a wide set of strategic, creative and technical services within the digital arena, ranging from online branding & experience design for corporate and consumer websites, to interactive content creation, games & online communitites, to content management solutions & intranets. Our client list includes the BBC, Red Bull, Getty Images, Warp Films, Nike Germany, Dentsu & SEGA Japan.

reception@lessrain.com
www.lessrain.com

How does your story begin? With a fish. *What was your favourite story as a child?* A German poem from the 19th century that begins with 'Dunkel war's, der Mond schien helle' ('Dark it was, the moon shone brightly'). The author is unknown. *What is the background to that story?* It's a silly poem, describing a very strange night. *What was the twist in the plot?* The twist is that every line is an oxymoron. I was fascinated by this. *Who are you at war with?* Rain in London. *Who or what are you in love with?* Less Rain in Tokyo. *What is the Holy Grail?* Nobody knows, that's the point. *Is your life an Odyssey or an Iliad?* Either way, as long as it's not a short story. *Biblical stories: what are your ten commandments?* We have only one: Nothing should be set in stone. *Ghost stories: what haunts you?* The deadlines under my bed. *Horror stories: what really scares you?* That alternate reality in which I never left my hometown. I have a Volvo estate, a terraced house, a family, a dog, and I design the local newspaper. *What's your kryptonite?* If you mean the green variety, it's definitely fish. *Who's your ideal audience?* Demanding. And forgiving. *What's a happy ending?* No ending is a happy one, it means the story is over. *Famous last line:* By when did you say you need this? *[Answers by Carsten]*

Destination Death
01.2006
The game has been created for the BBC Bitesize Revision website, and it is a German, French & Spanish language revision game for 11–14 year olds. We were asked to create a language revision game that can be skinned for 3 different languages – the rest was carte blanche. We chose a 'vampire' theme as it is quite popular to out target group, even amongst girls. We also chose an 'airport' sub-theme, as it offered a lot of possibilities to revise most of the foreign languages curriculum. The game is a point-and-click adventure that takes place in Germany, France or Spain, in the corresponding language. Players need to understand what is going on and act accordingly, aiming to finish the game as fast as they can.

00

01

02

03

04

05

06

07

08

04, 05
Less Rain Tokyo website

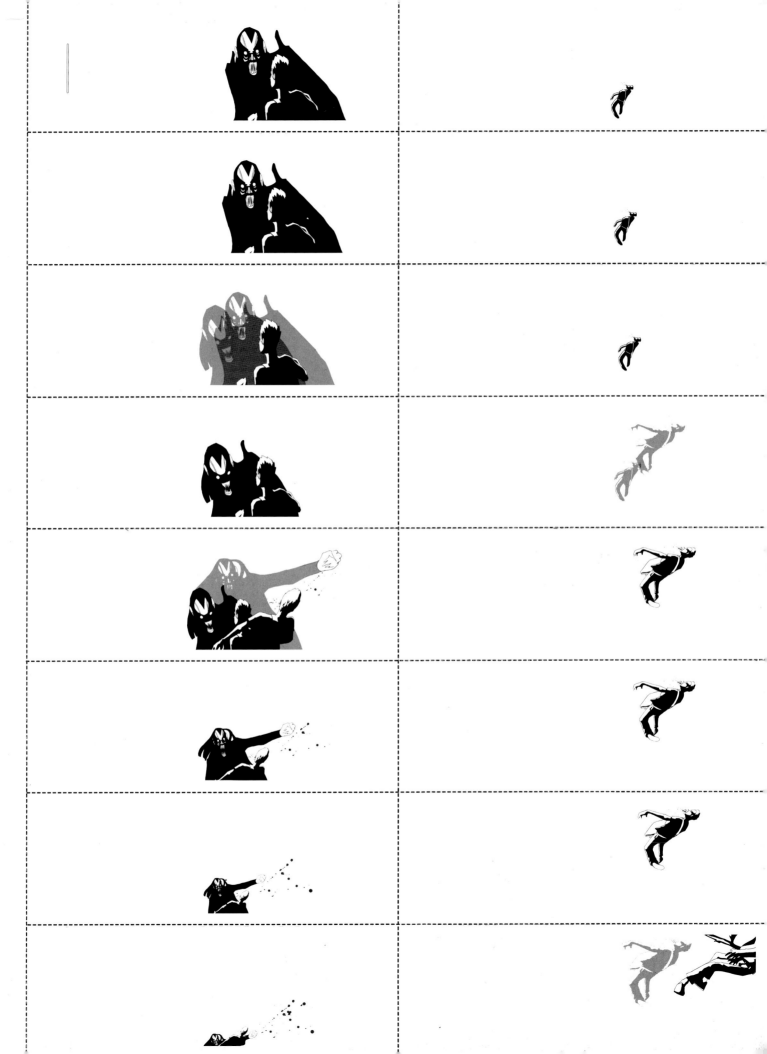

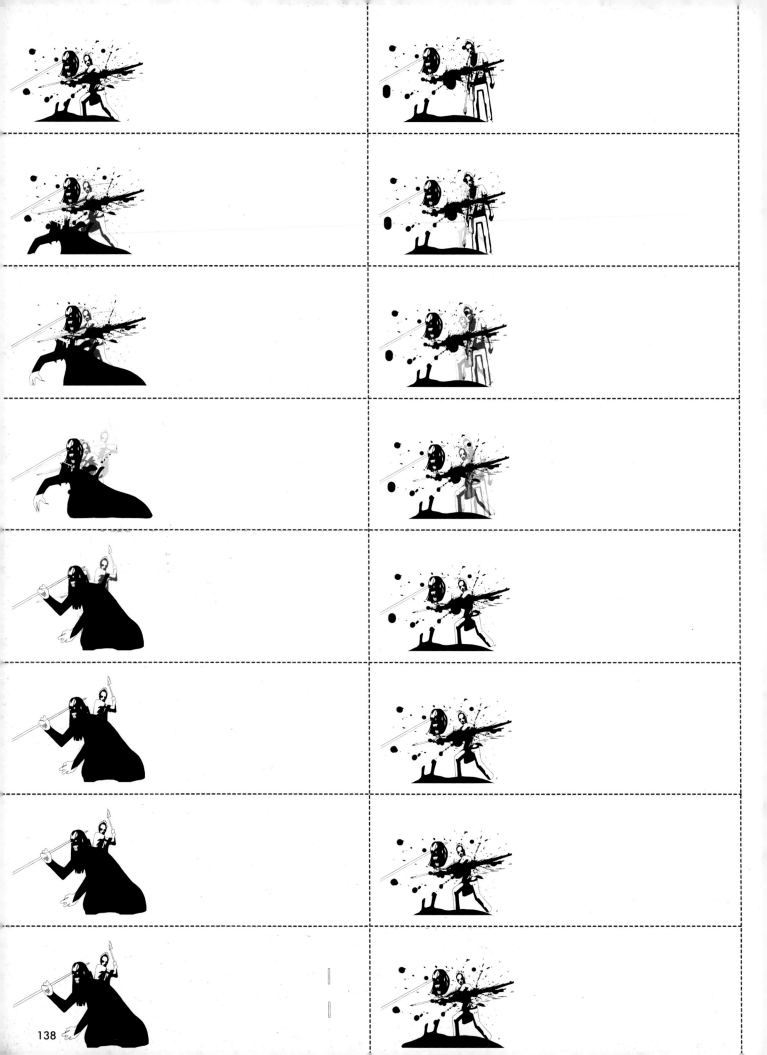

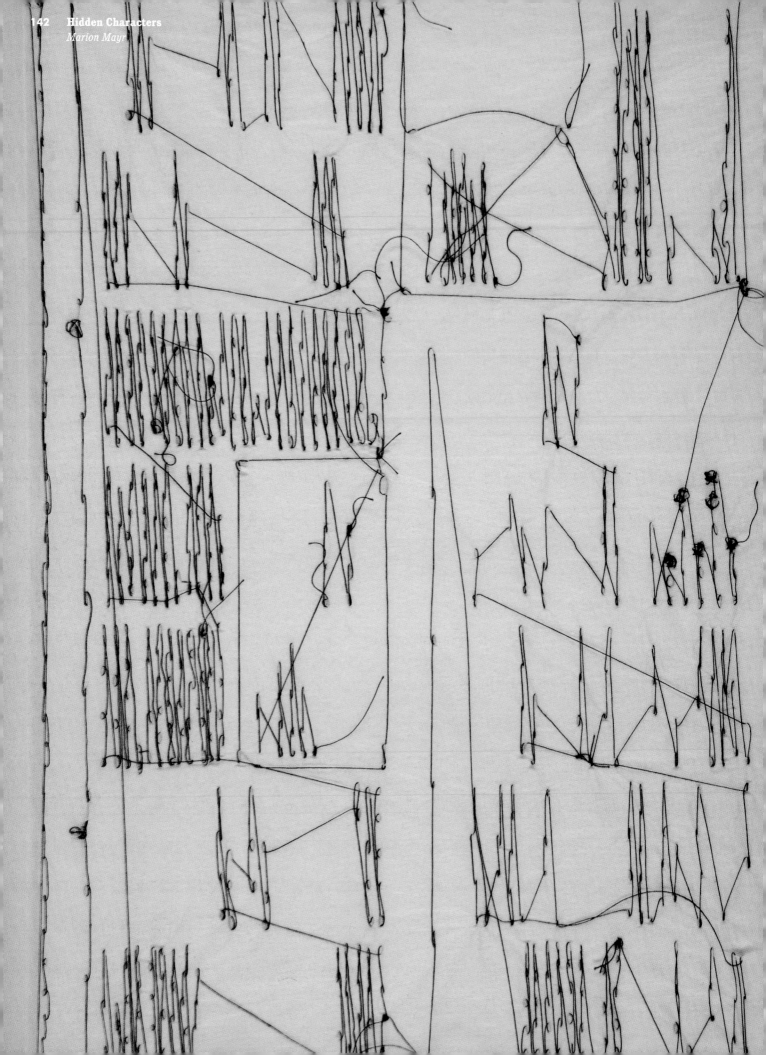

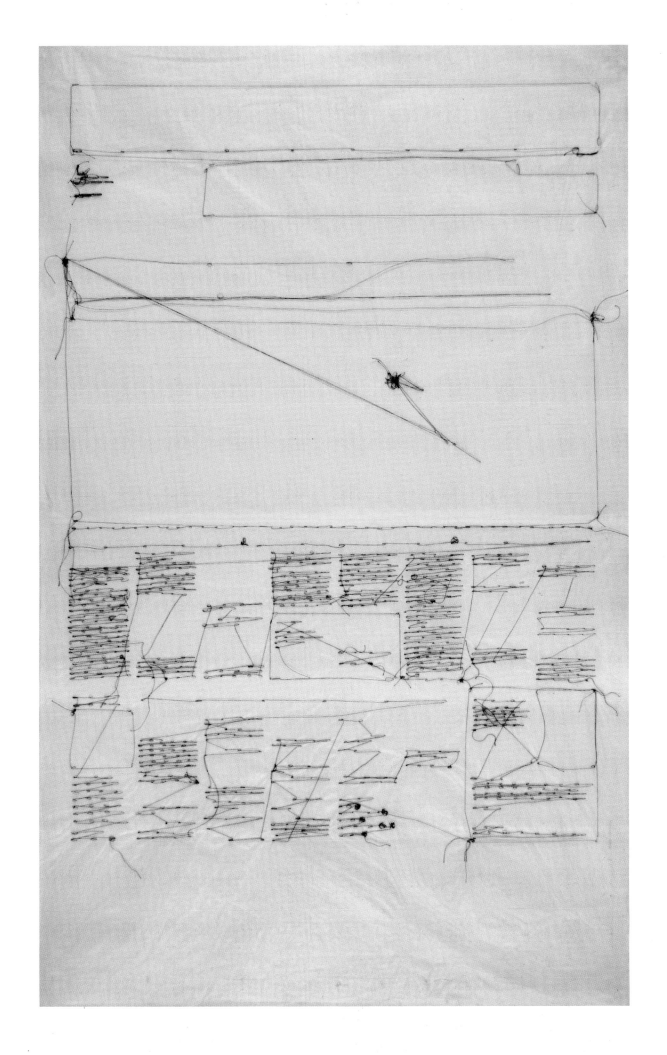

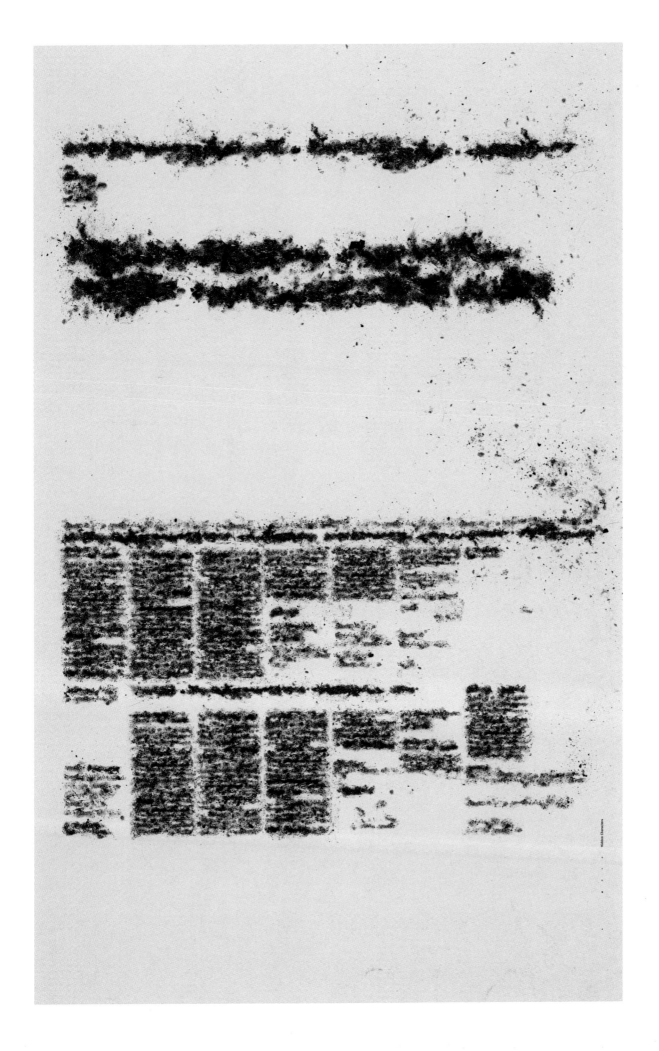

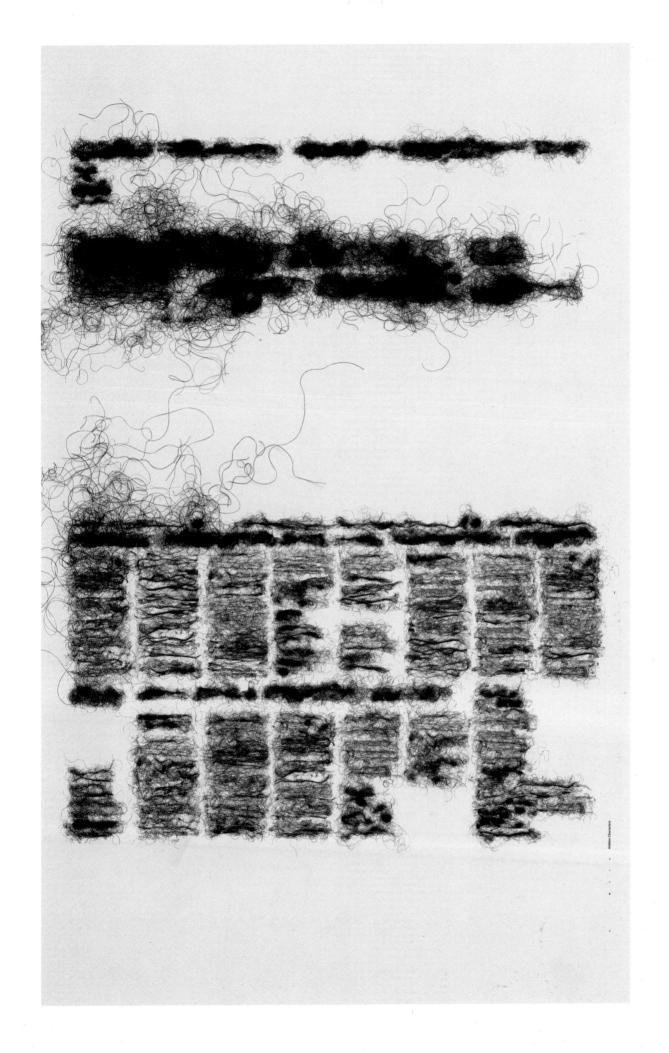

I have studied in Vienna and London. For the past five years I have been working freelance and part time as a graphic designer for several studios in Vienna, New York and London.

marion.mayr@gmx.at
maid.sonance.net

mapping my
th a thread.
: identity of
entity of the
res stories for an
: typography is an
vacuated memory.

er of different
idual reader
se messages
ypography as
ded to turn this
m a distance, it
nly a close view

How does your story begin? In a rabbit burrow. *What was your favourite story as a child?* The Cyclops scene from Homer's *Odyssey* and the scene *Die Wolfsschlucht* from *Der Freischütz und der Teufel*. *What is the background to that story?* Both are a little dark and frightening for a primary school girl. One was a record and the other one a tape. I used to just listen to these two scenes over and over again. I hardly ever listened to the other parts of the stories. *What was the twist in the plot?* I was sent to bed. *How would you define your character?* As a helicopter. Sometimes I am not able to land and sometimes I am not able to take off. *Who are the bad guys?* The ones who are not able to love themselves. *Who are the good guys?* The ones who are able to love themselves. *What is the character you most identify with?* The Brain from *Pinky And The Brain*. *What is the Holy Grail?* Chocolate. *In what form do the aliens appear?* Huge tomatoes. *Special effects? Do you use any?* 'Don't think, feeeeeeeeeeeel …' *What's your kryptonite?* Claustrophobia. *Who's your ideal audience?* You. *What's a happy ending?* Rainbows, butterflies, bunnies, pixies and a lot of chocolate ice-cream … *Famous last line:* 'The mediator between head and hands must be the heart.' (*Metropolis*, 1927)

00

01

02

03

04

05

06

07

08

06–08
The Origin of Letters by Means of Human Selection
Vienna, 2002
Book (156mm × 253mm, 80 pages), x-ray, linen chart (841mm × 1189mm), letters made of latex and plaster, 3 animations.
'My work interprets the expression "Organic Typography". I describe typography by means of the definition of life (growth, receptiveness to stimuli, motion, reproduction, metabolism) as if it was a living being. If there is optimum legibility and/or aesthetics, typography is

03
The Culinary Heritage of Austria: 100 Classic Dishes
Vienna, 2002
Cookery book. 300mm × 190mm, 360 pages, bilingual English and German, authors: Ewald Plachutta and Christoph Wagner, publisher: Deuticke Verlag, photos: C. Alessandri. Awards: Tokyo Type Directors Club 2003, Venus-Creativ Club Austria 2003, Die schönsten Bücher Österreichs 2003,

04, 05
Familienalbum
Vienna, 2004
Catalogue, 297mm × 210mm, 80 pages, fashion designer Mel Merio, 30 different photographers (e.g. Peter Rigaud, Udo Titz, Michael Dürr, Bernhard Musil, Klaus Mähring, Raphael Just …), Austrian celebrity models (e.g. Richard Dorfmeister, Fennesz, Electric Indigo, Hermes Phettberg, Twinnie, Patrick

se

4mm),
ral London
f Univers
d on central
gating through

Polly Morgan

A love of animals and desire to preserve them led Polly Morgan to learn taxidermy and since then she has gravitated towards making still lives with the animal as subject.

Her intention has never been to mimic the natural habitats of animals, as they are traditionally displayed, but to place them in less expected scenery. The scale and settings are often unnatural, but the animals are never anthropomorphised. Seeing them out of place encourages us to look at them as if for the first time; a rat sheds its association with horror and disease and can be rightly viewed as a beautiful animal.

Her first show was the unveiling of four phantasmagorical belljars, commissioned by Bistrotheque, on August 3rd 2005. Since then she has shown *Rest a Little on the Lap of Life,* which featured a white rat curled up in a champagne bowl glass and topped with a miniature crystal chandelier, in the London Zoo Art Fair (October 2005). She took part in 'Santa's Ghetto', the Banksy-curated group show alongside artists David Shrigley, Chris Cunningham and Jamie Hewlett in December 2005.

In March 2006 she will contribute work to the debut show of new Greek street gallery Laz Inc. She is currently working towards a solo show in summer/autumn 2006.

How does your story begin? In an ancient Scottish tower with a total stranger. *What was your favourite story as a child?* Something grisly and gruesome I'd written about twins, cliff edges, sleepwalking, mistaken identity and wrongful imprisonment. *What is the background to that story?* An obsession with twins and sleep activity. *What was the twist in the plot?* The bad prevailed, the good were assailed. *Who are the bad guys?* The rude. *Who are the good guys?* All the little animals. *Who is your hero or heroine?* Charlotte Church. *Who or what are you in love with?* Life. *What is the character you most identify with?* A London pigeon. *In what form do the aliens appear?* They come on two, four, six, eight or more legs. They fly, swim or creep about in the undergrowth. They appear in so many forms and I love them all. *Biblical stories: what are your ten commandments?* There's only one I need: Thou shalt not waste. *Horror stories: what really scares you?* The rather persistent dreams I have of holding babies that turn into rodents and wriggle out of my hands and get lost or crushed under furniture. *Special effects? Do you use any?* No. it's all real. *What's your kryptonite?* Bed. *Who's your ideal audience?* Creature-loving carnivores. *What's a happy ending?* Acceptance. *Famous last line:* But I haven't finished yet …

Aubade
11.2005

Love Bird in Mirror
Magpie and Diamond
Squirrel and Fly
Chicks on Coffin
08.2005
Commission for the restaurant/bar Bistrotheque in August 2005.

Still Life After Death
11.2005

Rest a Little on the Lap of Life
10.2005
A quote from a George Eliot poem called *In a London Drawing Room.* It's about the beauty of things we take for granted or even despise.

00

01

02

03

04

05

06

07

08

00
Polly Morgan

01
Owl
Work in progress. To be shown in March

02
Pigeon
The first few stages of 'mounting' a bird.

04, 05
After Death, Still Life
02.2006

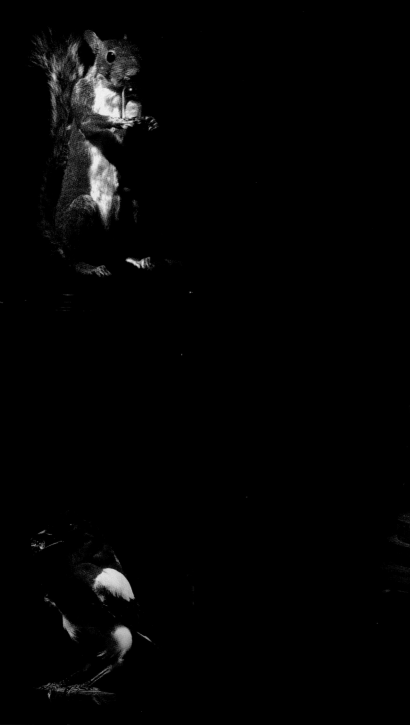

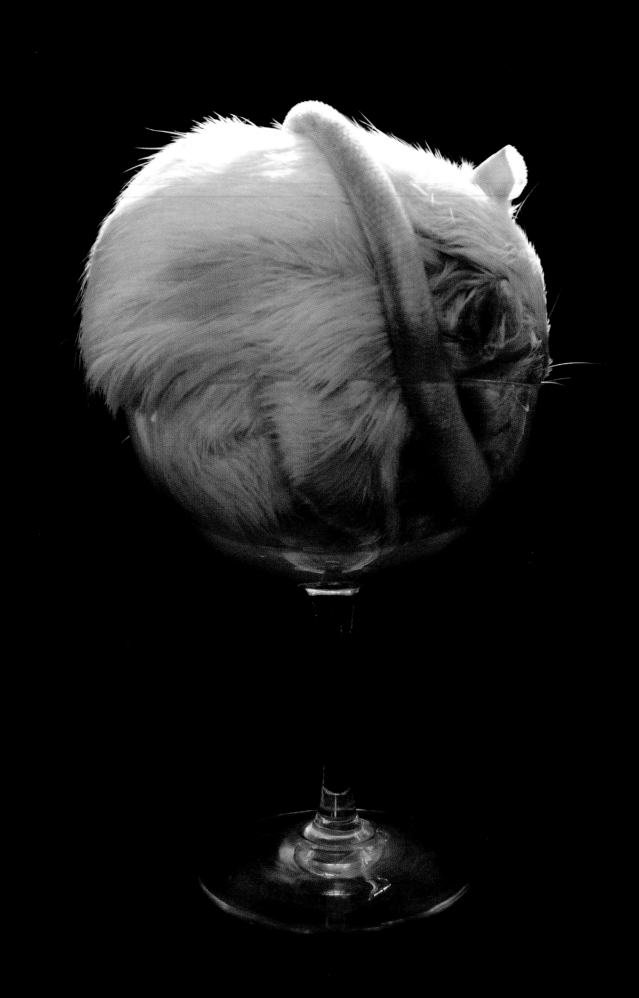

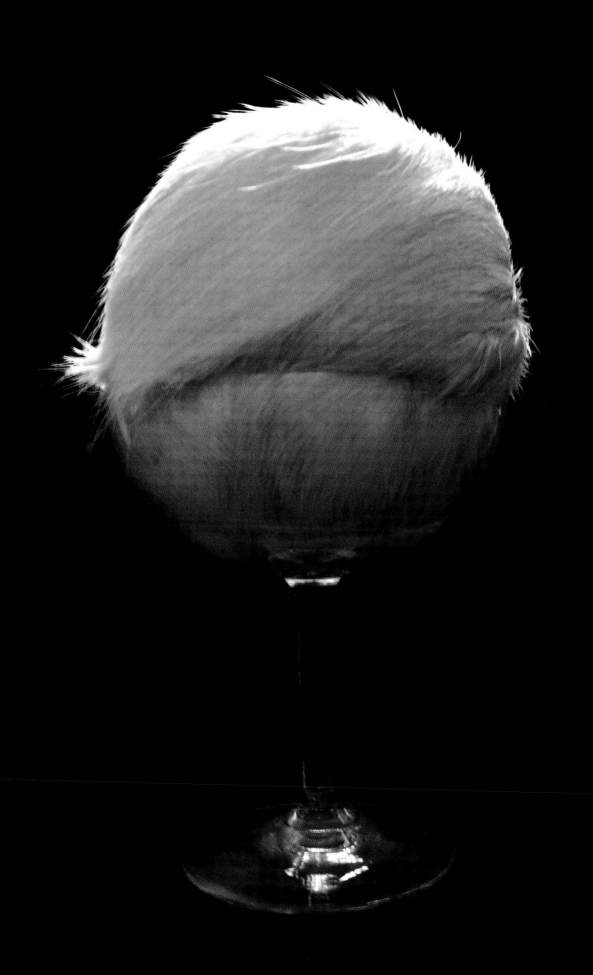

)
need to
th others
evance
great
nalizing
onnection

which we
everyday,
per man,
em to that
tuation
ge their

Megan Olinger spent her early years in the suburbs of Chicago, where she was never bored, due to all the forts to build and games to invent with her Pipi Longstocking-ish little sister and the other latchkey kids in the neighborhood. She moved to the countryside of Iowa at age 13. Thankful for the years spent driving on gravel roads, she stayed in the Midwest and attended the University of Wisconsin, Madison. After school, she began working as a Camera Assistant on independent films and commercials. Megan moved to Hong Kong with her family in 2002. She continues to live in Hong Kong and feels blessed to have many places to call home. With aspirations of cinematography, Meg is inspired by the cinematic moments in every day life. 'Photographically capturing the instant when the back story is understood, and the future can be inferred through the perspective of the viewer, and the audience is made conscious of the weave of individual, yet connected, narratives unfolding simultaneously, is the moment storytelling becomes excitingly apparent.'

meganolinger@gmail.com

How does your story begin? My story be... duplex in a suburb. Zoom in through rays... two little girls building a rocket out of a ... helped drag out of the furniture store dur... **story as a child?** *The Sneetches* by Dr. Se... film, *Charlie And The Chocolate Factory.* W... **story?** Some Sneetches have stars on the... Sneetches with stars think they are far b... not invite the ones with out to their hotd... **in the plot?** Sylvester McMonkey McBea... magnificent star on and star off machine!... look the same and none can remember if ... not. **Who or what are you in love with?** T... **effects? Do you use any?** I suppose all ef... to learn how to use a computer so I can tr... only effects I know how to do are in came... **a happy ending?** 'And they lived happily e... dance number at the end. **Famous last lin...**

00

01

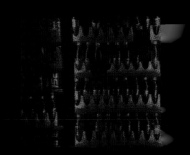

02

03

04

05

06

07

08

03, 04
Man on escalator
Woman on escalator
2000
'This could be Vancouver or anywhere.'
35mm black & white reversal

05
Ashley
2003
Hong Kong series. 35mm colour prints

06, 07, 08
Bow your head
Red laundry
Burning time
2004
Red Film series.
35mm colour reversal

rtising,

Mike Joyce / Stereotype

Mike Joyce is the founder of Stereotype Design in New York City, specializing in projects for the music industry. He has designed CD packaging for established artists and upstarts, from Iggy Pop and Natalie Merchant to Fall Out Boy and Robbers on High Street. Mike has also designed countless T-shirts for bands like The Strokes, The All American Rejects and Maroon 5, and has produced books for Tony Hawk and KISS. Stereotype's work has been featured in publications such as *IdN*, *Print*, *Communication Arts*, *HOW*, *Rolling Stone*, *Plus 81* and *New York* magazine. Exhibitions include the AIGA 365, Type Directors Club, the One Show, the Art Directors Club's first *Young Guns* show, and the Permanent Collection of the Library of Congress. In 2004 Mike was selected to co-chair the Art Directors Club's *Young Guns 4*. He also teaches typography and design to third and fourth year students at the School of Visual Arts and may be the only graphic designer with absolutely no interest in collecting sneakers.

How does your story begin? A boy is born in Troy, NY. *How would you define your character?* Flawed. *Who are the bad guys?* The Yankees. *Who are the good guys?* The Yankees. *Who is your hero or heroine?* Dr Kevorkian. *Who are you at war with?* The IRS. *Who or what are you in love with?* New York. *What is the character you most identify with?* Number Six. *If your life was turned into a Hollywood movie, who would you like to play your role?* Edward Norton. *What is the Holy Grail?* A myth. *Is your life an Odyssey or an Iliad?* An Odyssey. *In what form do the aliens appear?* Probably exactly like the Great Gazoo. *Biblical stories: what are your ten commandments?* Wake up; brush teeth; shower; design; invoice; eat; design; drink; sleep; repeat. *Ghost stories: what haunts you?* High school chemistry. *Horror stories: what really scares you?* Religion and Leatherface. *Do you spy on other people's work? Who do you spy on?* Yes. Lester Beall and Reid Miles. *Special effects? Do you use any?* Helvetica. *What's your kryptonite?* Weddings. *Who's your ideal audience?* The 16–64 demographic. *What's a happy ending?* Something you can get in Chinatown. *Famous last line:* 'For a moment there, I thought we were in trouble.'

Untitled
A film has a life to it that can't be be summed up in words. The dialogue, performances, direction, and cinematography come together to create something that is unique to film. A movie has an intangible pulse to it – something we all respond to, whether it be comedy, drama, action, or horror. The following spreads showcase what happens when these films are summed up in one brief and broken sentence for television and video guides. Sometimes funny, sometimes confusing, these descriptions never come close in capturing the spirit and soul of the film in its original and intended medium. Stereotype movie T-shirts are now available at www.2ktshirts.com

00

01

02

03

04

05

06

07

08

00
Mike Joyce

01
25 Above Water
Hurricane Katrina Relief & Rescue poster

02
The All American Rejects
Dirty Little Secret T-shirt.
Client: Zambooie

03
Fall Out Boy Show Poster
Client: Fuelled By Ramen

04
Floor Jack
Transistor CD package.
Client: Maggadee Records

05
Gorillaz Invasion Tour Poster
Client: Virgin Records

06
Iggy Pop
Skull Ring CD package.
Client: Virgin Records

07
Rock 'n Roll Soldiers
So Many Musicians To Kill T-shirt.
Client: Atlantic Records

08
Swiss Modern T-shirt
Client: 2K

An ambitious Cuban refugee obsesses over his sister's love life and becomes the cocaine king of Miami (1983).
★★★

A pilot afraid to fly follows his stewardess ex-girlfriend and must take over for plane's poisoned crew (1980).
★★

A dirty dog assists a tidy detective link California beach-town foul play to a drug-money laundry (1989).
★★

A New Jersey teen moves to California, meets bullies and learns karate from a handyman (1984).
★★★

The beer-drinking manager of a peewee team bribes a girl pitcher to lead his ragtag losers (1976). ★★⅃

The trendy teen scene in California includes a party-animal surfer, a pregnant girl and a fast food clerk (1982). ★★

Philadelphia south-paw finds soul mate in pet shop, trains with raw meat and gets a shot at the title (1976). ★★★★

A truck driver woos a country singer and fights bare-knuckled brawls, egged on by his orangutan (1978).

Two brothers seeking redemption set out to re-enlist members of their defunct band for honest pay (1980).
★★★

Oddballs and gophers undermine a country-club caddy determined to win a full college scholarship (1980).
★★★⍟

Nature and hillbillies humble four Atlanta businessmen on a trip in the Appalachian backwoods (1972).
★★★★

Hippies encounter a family of cannibals, who chase them with chainsaws and other lethal tools (1974).
★★★⯪

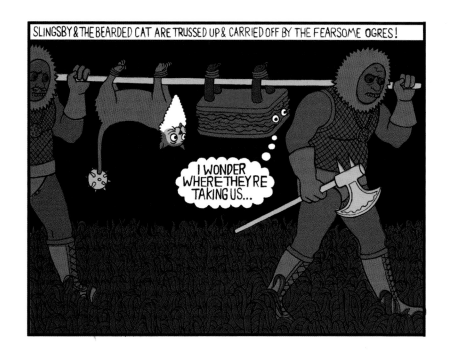

00

01

02

Graduated from The Royal College Of Art in 1998 and began working as a freelance illustrator with regular editorial work for magazines such as *Sleaze Nation*, *Dazed & Confused* and *The Face*. In 1999 he began producing work for Silas & Maria, including catalogue design and illustration, a multitude of T-shirt designs, posters and large scale store art for the Silas & Maria stores in Japan. He also started working for a wide range of other clothing companies including Levi Strauss, Stüssy and Gimme Five. 2003 saw the launch of the book *Where Is Silas?*, to which he contributed 15 pages of drawings. He has also created large-scale installation art for La Condition Publique in Roubaix, France and a limited edition book for Crespi textiles, Milan. In early March 2005 Amos Toys, Silas' sister company, released a comic book, *Tales From Greenfuzz* written & illustrated by Will, and a toy design, *Helmut The Hot Dog Man*. In 2005, he was invited to Japan to hold his exhibition with Susumu Mukai at Beams T Tokyo. He is currently working on his next comic book. His new toys, *Kleptikos & Periwinkle: The Kebab Brothers* from Amos are to be released in January 2006.

www.willsweeney.com

How does your story begin? On the streets of Rastapopolis, a city inhabited by various vegetables, sandwiches, labradors and owls. **What was your favourite story as a child?** The Three Robbers. **What is the background to that story?** As far as I can remember, there are three robbers. One has a blunderbuss, one has some pepper spray and the other an axe. They are planning some shenanigans. **How would you define your character?** There are many characters in *Tales From Greenfuzz*, but the protagonist is Slingsby Sandwich, an innocent, everyday kind of sandwich who works in a bank **Who are the bad guys?** The notorious Nutwood Gang, led by Helmut Von Weinerschnitzel. **In what form do the aliens appear?** Hopefully enormous black and red robots playing electric guitars and mesmerising the whole world with their cosmic vortex of psychedelic sounds. **Horror stories: what really scares you?** Impalement, the rack, being broken at the wheel, Nazi experiments on concentration camp internees, Abu Ghraib prison, Guantánamo Bay. **Special effects? Do you use any?** Latex, foam rubber, dry ice, fake blood, corpse paint. **What's your kryptonite?** Crème de menthe. **Who's your ideal audience?** Really cool, famous, sexy and intelligent people. **What's a happy ending?** Meeting the audience. **Famous last line:** 'Repo Man's always intense!'

03

04

05

06

02
Tales From Greenfuzz
Comic book cover. *TFG* is a story concerning a living sandwich and an evil gang of fast food characters. *Tales From Greenfuzz* issue 2 will be published by Amos novelties soon.

03
Dark Wave
Still from the music video *Dark Wave* by Stephen Malkmus & The Jicks.

04
Saturday Night

05
The Shit Hits The Fan

06
The White Stripes

ZK's files include passports from the USA and Switzerland, a childhood of palm trees, Alps and suburbs, an abandoned double major, a three-year hideout in the hills outside Los Angeles and a degree from CalArts. Kyes' work has been described as 'wrestling the bulky corpus of the known to the ground'. His work takes an experimental position in graphic design, using writing as its foundation and linking to external disciplines such as art-history and architecture.

Kyes was the first student to be awarded by the Art Directors Club Hall of Fame. In 2005 he won the annual Creative Futures prize and The Independent named him one of the 'brightest stars in creation'. In 2006 Kemistry Gallery held a solo exhibition of his work, *All That Is Solid Melts Into Air*.

Zak Kyes currently lives in London. He works out of his studio Zak Group in Shoreditch, East London.

studio@zak.to
www.zak.to

How does your story begin? In the novel form, with the first lines from my favourite novels: **What is the background to that story?** I wake up and call B. Andy Warhol, *The Philosophy of Andy Warhol*. **What was the twist in the plot?** Seeing comes before words. John Berger, *Ways of Seeing*. **How would you define your character?** It was a pleasure to burn. Ray Bradbury, *Fahrenheit 451*. **Who are the bad guys?** I live on Earth at present, and I don't know what I am. R. Buckminster Fuller, *I Seem To Be a Verb*. **Who or what are you in love with?** The sun shone, having no alternative, on the nothing new. Samuel Beckett, *Murphy*. **What is the Holy Grail?** Mother died today. Albert Camus, *The Stranger*. **Is your life an Odyssey or an Iliad?** If you really want to hear about it, the first thing you'll probably want to know is where I was born, and what my lousy childhood was like, and how my parents were occupied and all before they had me, and all that David Copperfield kind of crap, but I don't feel like going into it, if you want to know the truth. J.D. Salinger, *The Catcher in the Rye*. **Special effects? Do you use any?** Many years later, as he faced the firing squad, Colonel Aureliano Buendía was to remember that distant afternoon when his father took him to discover ice. Gabriel García Márquez, *One Hundred Years of Solitude*. **Famous last line:** The end.

nOulipo (after Georges Perec)
Poster for nOulipo, a conference on the French experimental writing group Oulipo. Oulipo (Ouvroir de Littérature Potentielle) became renowned for their use of constraint.

Pornographics / ArtSlut
Pornographics poster for symposium on pornography in contemporary culture. All text is extracted from subject headers of pornographic spam emails.

Fall / 02.11.06
The typographic noise from a recent London performance by The Fall.

All That Is Solid Melts Into Air
Exhibition at Kemistry Gallery, London 2006.

00

01

02

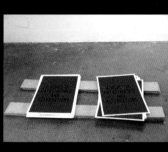

03

04

05

06

07

08

00
Zak Kyes

01
Oh Astro Hello World
CD package for sonic artist Jane Dowe's album *Oh Astro Hello World*. Cover artwork created by running pop songs through an Ampex ADO-100 and 3D rendering software.

02
No More of This Shit
CalArts graduate pins.

03
The Living History Project
08.2005
Poster series for Kim Schoen's exhibition *Living History Project*.

04
Superstudio: A Catalog In Flux
A Catalog In Flux reflects Superstudio's architectural 'thought experiments' in the mid '60s, such as the *Continuous Monument*, a single dystopian superstructure encircling the globe.

05
PLAN 8
Identity for fashion collective PLAN 8. Composed of interchangeable typographic rings and customized typeface.

06
Untitled Proposal (Prada)
From a proposal for a fashion identity with bespoke typeface.

07, 08
The Institute for Words and Pictures
The *IFW&P* is a fictionalized paperback document of the history, politics and identity of CalArts during the late 1980s.

noulipo:
a 2 day public meditation on the future of constraints in writing
Organized by Matias Viegener & Christine Wertheim
Sponsored by The Annenberg Foundation and CalArts MFA Writing Program

October 28th & 29th, 2005
at REDCAT, The Roy and Edna Disney | CalArts Theater in downtown Los Angeles.
Six daytime panels and two evening readings, plus public workshops.
More info: www.redcat.org, e-mail: noulipo@gmail.com

Participants
Caroline Bergvall, Christian Bök, Johanna Drucker, Paul Fournel, Tan Lin, Harry Mathews, Bernadette Mayer, Ian Monk, Harryette Mullen, Doug Nufer, Vanessa Place, Janet Sarbanes, Brian Kim Stefans, Juliana Spahr, Rodrigo Toscano

I'll s/nd you info on th/ noulipo conf/r/nc/ today (sorry I m/ant to do that y/st/rday). Oulipo is th/ Fr/nch /xp/rim/ntal writing group that has b/com/ r/nown/d for /xploring th/ us/ of constraint. Th/ir b/st-known m/mb/r is p/rhaps G/org/s P/r/c, who wrot/ *Lif/, A Us/r's Manual*, and th/ book that b/st illustrat/s th/ir prin-cipl/s is his disapp/aranc/ nov/l, *A Void*, which is a d/t/ctiv/ story tracing th/ lif/ of a disapp/ar/d writ/r, in which h/ n/v/r onc/ us/s any words with th/ l/tt/r "/." W/ put th/ n at th/ b/ginning of th/ titl/ to signify both n/w and th/ id/a of math or alg/bra, as in "l/t x = 1." (A lot of noulipo's /xp/rim/nts ar/ influ/nc/d by math. N+7 is a con-straint which substitut/s all th/ nouns in a t/xt with th/ 7th noun b/low it in th/ dictionary.) A constraint is a sort of limiting d/sign principl/ that a writ/r assigns hims/lf to guid/ him in cr/ating an /xp/rim/ntal t/xt, for /xampl/: to writ/ /v/ry word in a po/m in alphab/tical ord/r (as in "And B/caus/ Carla…")

I can't r/ally /xplain our logic for choosing th/ Ouchi Illusion* /xc/pt that Op Art s//ms lik/ a good match – Oulipians hav/ d/scrib/d th/m-s/lv/s as "rats who build th/ maz/ from which th/y plan to /scap/." (Th/ history of th/ Ouchi at HTTP://MATHWORLD.WOLFRAM.COM/OUCHIILLUSION.HTML).

Mor/ info: noulipo is th/ s/cond annual /xp/rim/ntal writing /v/nt to b/ h/ld at R/DCAT, th/ Roy and /dna Disn/y | CalArts Th/at/r in down-town Los Ang/l/s. It tak/s plac/ on th/ w//k/nd of Octob/r 28th and 29th, 2005. *n*oulipo puts n/w and /stablish/d writ/rs into dialogu/ about issu/s in cont/mporary writing and its r/lations to /v/ryday lif/.

This y/ar our focus is on th/ l/gacy of th/ Fr/nch lit/rary group Oulipo, inviting a conv/rsation b/tw//n th/ originators of this major /xp/rim/n-tal coll/ctiv/ and som/ of th/ir /nglish sp/aking count/rparts and h/irs. Our aim is to discuss curr/nts in cont/mporary writing that combin/ strat/gi/s d/v/lop/d by m/mb/rs of Oulipo with oth/r t/chniqu/s, to mov/ b/yond an oppositional id/a of form and d/v/lop n/w mod/s of wordwork that chall/ng/ structur/s of domination by s/riously play-ing with th/ wor(l)d.

CalArts' downtown center for innovative visual, performing and media arts at the corner of 2nd and Hope Streets in the Walt Disney Concert Hall complex. 631 W 2nd Street, Los Angeles, CA 90012 / www.redcat.org / tel: 213-237-2800

REDCAT's 2005-06 Season Sponsors:
LA WEEKLY

Graphic Design: Zak Kyis (Zak Group)
Text: Matias Vi/g/e/r

ARE YOU ALONE? ALL THE BOND GIRLS AND GUYS EXPOSED, AMAZING GLORY HOLE ACTION, MOST AMAZING WEBCAM COCK SLOBBERS YOU'VE SEEN! APPEALING TO HOT ONES, BE A BETTER LOVER, GET THE COCK YOUR GODDESS CRAVES, HOT CUNTS WORKING FROM HOME, BETTER SEX LIFE, BIG TIT PATROL, BIGGER WIENER, BULLFROG FETISHISTS & BEYOND, FW: BETTER SEX: ANYTIME YOU WANT IT, CHEATING HOUSEWIFE WHORES, DETAILED GUIDE ON HOW TO SEDUCE A GIRL, CAN YOU REALLY DRILL HER? DO YOU MEASURE UP, DRIVE MEN OR WOMEN WILD, TALKING DIRTY! ERECTION IN 15 MINUTES, YOUNG BEAVERS WITH TIGHT ASSHOLES, TRY POWERFUL ERECTIONS THROUGH CHEMISTRY, EXPERIENCE YOUR SEXUAL PEAK, FREE SEX, FRESH GIRLS GOING ANAL, RE: FREE PORN, GIRLS WANT IT BIGGER! GIVE THE GIRL WHAT SHE NEEDS, SEXY BOYS WAITING FOR YOU, INEBRIATED COLLEGE SLUTS FLASHING THE CAMERA, MY PARENTS ARE GONE FOR THE WEEKEND! NOW YOU CAN BE MORE

[1] A panel discussion on the role of pornography in shaping contemporary culture, sexuality, gender relations, and *art practice.*

[2] Panelists:
Juliet MacCannell,
UC IRVINE
Constance Penley,
UC SANTA BARBARA
William Jones,
FILMMAKER
Matias Viegener,
CALARTS

ARTSLUT: A collection of 25 years of handmade sex fetish videos by LA artists from 1975 - 2004 curated by Dave Burns and Bruce Yonemoto.

Organized By:
Janet Sarbanes,
Matias Viegener and
Christine Wertheim.

Graphic Design:
ZK/GC/CP
CalArts 2005

Screenprint:
UnitTwentyFive
Print Studio
unittwentyfive.com

THERE'S ALWAYS WORK IN PROGRESS I YOU'RE COULDA HAD A LIFE WORK COULDA HAD A COULDA WIFE HE A LIFE WORK COULDA SAID — THERE'S ALWAYS A LIFE SOMEONE ROUND ME — NOT HER — YOU ROUND WANNER — AND YOU SAY YOUR ROUND WANNER I'VE NEVER FELT LIKE THIS WANNER WITH I ANYONE FELT ELSE — SO YOU MOAN ALL DAY ANYONE IT YOU'RE A MOANER — EER GET THE TIME TOGETHER — M ANER NEVER WORK IN PROGRESS TOGETHER — IT IS THE NEVER — IN PROGRESS FLAVOUR OF IT OUTSIDERNESS YOU DUE ABOUT 2026 OUTSIDERNESS YOU WANNER.

Ou-ba-po
Stephen Preston

Comics break free of their constraints: Steven Preston reflects on the essence of comic strip narrative and how artists such as Matt Madden, Jochen Gerner and Killoffer are challenging our notions of narrative and storytelling.

Comics are a medium, not a genre. While the vast majority of this medium is formulaic rubbish decorated by slapstick superheroes, throughout its history there has been a strong seam of ground-breaking work buried among the silly masks and movie tie-ins. George Herriman's *Krazy Kat* strips drawn in the twenties and thirties are still so inventive, so far ahead of their time that only now, some sixty years after their creator's death, they are being re-discovered and appraised for the true works of art they clearly are.

As this is a piece of writing about comics I am obliged by statute of law to inform you (in case you didn't know) that in 2001 cartoonist Chris Ware was awarded the Guardian's First Book Award for *Jimmy Corrigan*. Just as if it were a 'real' book. The Graphic Novel was coming of age. Not just with the work of Chris Ware, but also with that of Art Spiegelman, Daniel Clowes, Charles Burns, Jessica Abel, Jamie & Gilbert Hernandez, David B, Marjane Satrapi, Joe Sacco and Jason and many, many others. There is probably more inventive and intelligent work being produced by cartoonists now than at any other time since the dawn of time. Probably.

What makes a comic anyway? It's not putting pictures and words together to create some kind of narrative. If that was the case, then David Shrigley would be a cartoonist. But he isn't. Neither is Raymond Pettibon. Or Marcel Dzama.

No, what makes a comic a comic is the idea of *sequence*. Image A plus image B plus image C, multiplied to the power of words equals *comic* (or approximately that). The sequence makes the comic strip move through space and time. A comic strip is a map of time. Usually this sequence follows a pretty straight line, but the map is not always easy to follow. Luckily there are signposts. As well as the 'panels' (which keep the pictures from bumping into one another) the cartoonist has other happy tools to help him tell his story: word balloons, thought bubbles, motion lines, squiggly lines emanating from a character's head. Stuff like that. Sweat beads. Stink waves. All of these devices are so much a part of our shared visual pictographic language that merely to see

them on a page is enough. We all get it. These simple symbols, these emanations, say more than words can. They are literally pictures that speak.

* * *

American cartoonist Matt Madden has recently published *Exercises in Style – 99 Ways to Tell a Story* in which he takes a rather dull one page comic strip story (man gets up from his desk and walks through his apartment towards the fridge; on his way, he is briefly distracted by his wife, who asks him the time; he tells her; upon arrival in the kitchen he pauses before the fridge's open door; he's forgotten what he was looking for) and proceeds to re-tell it. Ninety-nine times, in ninety-nine different ways, different tenses, different points of view, different comics styles (superhero, horror …) Forwards. Backwards. Ninety-nine different ways to tell the same little story.

Steven Preston: What was your initial inspiration for doing this book? Matt Madden: I discovered Raymond Queneau's *Exercises in Style* (1947) when I was working in a bookstore in Ann Arbor, Michigan, in the early nineties. It's a prose book that retells the same banal anecdote ninety nine times using different styles, voices, and rhetorical strategies. There's a haiku version, a telegraph version, a pig Latin version, and so on. I was just starting to draw comics and I was immersing myself in the history and the study of the medium so it struck me almost immediately that the concept of the book would apply really well to comics. In addition to text I would have images to play with as well as the grammar and punctuation of comics, its panel borders, gutters, word balloons, sound effects, and so on. ***Steven: Your work has parallels with Ou-Ba-Po in France. How would you define Ou-Ba-Po and what are the differences between what they are doing and Exercises in Style?*** Matt: OuLiPo (*Ouvroir de la Littérature Potentielle*, or Workshop for Potential Literature), the parent group of Ou-Ba-Po, describe themselves as 'mice who build the maze from which they propose to escape' and that's a nice summary of the project. Ou-Ba-Po is involved in creating comics by setting themselves rules and constraints to follow: comics palindromes, comics where faces can never be shown, where multiple storylines can be followed across the page, and so on. *Exercises in Style* has a constraint in that each variation has to tell the same basic story, but it is also different in that it is a series of variations on a theme. Queneau was originally inspired by a performance of Bach's *Art of the Fugue,* a group of eighteen fugues and canons based on a simple theme. In a way *Exercises* *in Style* exhibits the opposite of the typical Ou-Ba-Po constraint: whereas usually the idea is to choose a formal constraint in order to generate new content, in the case of *Exercises in Style* you could say that I am constraining content in order to free up form. Still, in the end they are very closely related in their interest in formal experimentation and the attitude of serious playfulness.

Steven: Your book is witty, thought provoking and genuinely funny. It must have been a lot of fun to do. And that is partly what bothers me about Ou-Ba-Po. That it's a way for cartoonists to play in public. It's not really too serious. Do you agree with this or do you believe that these exercises can really push comics in new directions? Matt: I believe both statements to be true depending on the situation and the work. Some Ou-Ba-Po (and, indeed, OuLiPo) work is pretty slight, while some is exciting and challenging and allows you to glimpse new vistas opening in the medium (I admit there aren't many of those yet, but there are a few). However, I don't think it's useful, or possible, for that matter, to separate out the 'deep' from the playful stuff. They are part and parcel of a larger project that involves play and experimentation in the service of both results you point to, fun and innovation. Sometimes those results are surprisingly rich and engaging, sometimes they aren't, but even

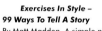

**Exercises In Style –
99 Ways To Tell A Story**
By Matt Madden. A simple narrative is told and re-told, in ninety-nine different ways.

'Ou-Ba-Po is involved in creating comics by setting themselves rules and constraints to follow: comics palindromes, comics where faces can never be shown, where multiple storylines can be followed across the page, and so on.'

185

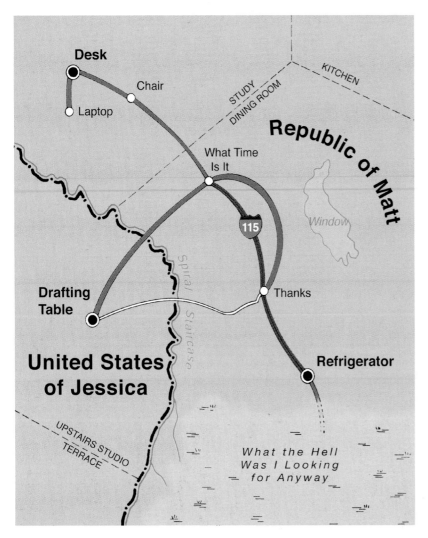

**Exercises In Style –
99 Ways To Tell A Story**
By Matt Madden. The execution
of the basic narrative can depart
hugely from conventional comics,
playing with style and graphic
vernacular.

the slighter experiments might inspire someone else to take an idea to a higher level. **Steven: Has this project had an effect on your other comics work? Are you now finding that working with constraints has changed your creative approach?** Matt: In a general sense, yes, *Exercises in Style* has had an enormous effect on my other work. It's hard to point to specific examples of that influence, though, and more importantly it's impossible for me to separate my work on *Exercises in Style* from my immersion in Ou-Ba-Po, OuLiPo, and constrained art in general over the last ten years. Almost everything on my slate right now is based on constraints: I just finished a story using a mathematical structure Georges Perec used called a 3×3 Greco-Latin bi-square (it will appear in a new Fantagraphics anthology called *Hotwire,* due in the spring). I'm working on a comics pantoum and a crab canon comic, a poetic and a musical form, respectively.

Steven: Can you recommend any Ou-Ba-Po related comics available to English-speaking readers?
Matt: There have been no translations of 'official' Ou-Ba-Po works in English yet (although the Ou-Ba-Po has more or less declared *Exercises in Style* to be an Ou-Ba-Po work), but there are lots of works out there that use constraints to one degree or another. Minicomics in general are a great source for formal experimentation. In the UK you can check out www.bugpowder.com for more info. My own series, *A Fine Mess,* features a number of constrained comics. Number two is available now and number three, a thirty-two-page palindrome comic, is forthcoming. I also have works in the anthologies Rosetta, Hotwire, and Blurred Vision. Killoffer is an Ou-Ba-Po member and his book *676 Apparitions of Killoffer* (Typocrat) is sort of quasi-Ou-Ba-Po work. Lewis Trondheim is another Ou-Ba-Po member who has been translated. His Fantagraphics series *The Nimrod* features a lot of formally playful short strips. Jason Shiga has done interesting stuff using math and branching narratives (www.shigabooks.com). There are several 'best of' collections of 24 Hour Comics, where you have to write and draw twenty-four pages in twenty-four hours (About Comics). Tom Motley has a lot of great, funny, experimental comics inspired by OuLiPo and surrealist games (minicomics). Luc and François Schuiten's *Nogegon*, a palindromic graphic novel published in English by Humanoids Publishing. Peter Blegvad's *Leviathan* is always an engaging read and occasionally draws from the OuLiPo pool among many other esoteric sources. The UK anthology *Test-Tube Comics* only put out one issue, called *Sentence,* but it features cartoonists doing some very interesting comics using only one sentence as their text.

*   *   *

Ou-Ba-Po stands for *Ouvrir de la Bande Desinee Potentielle.* Workshop for Potential Comics. Formed in Paris in 1992 by members of the comics collective L'Association: David B, JC Menu, Killoffer, Lewis Trondheim, Matt Konture and Stanislas. Taking their inspiration (and name) from an obscure French literary movement called OuLiPo (Workshop blah blah Literature). Spawned from the unlikely friendship between a writer (Raymond Queneau) and a mathematician (Francois Le Lionnais), OuLiPo sought, by imposing a series of often mathematically determined rules ('constraints') to open up new possibilities for creating literature (Queneau also published a book called *Exercises in Style,* in which he took a rather dull short prose story and proceeded to re-tell it. Niney-nine times …)

The artists behind Ou-Ba-Po felt alienated from the mainstream French comics industry (which subsists largely on sci-fi, fantasy and adventure stories) and this led them to form L'Association. Since its inception they have published dozens of graphic novels as well as the anthology series *Lapin* and an on-going series of Ou-Ba-Po projects, *Oupus.* Ou-Ba-Po takes the same idea of applying constraints to squeeze and twist comic-strips into strange new shapes. Strips that read left-to-right and right-to-left, strips that intersect with other strips like a crossword puzzle, strips that take panels from other strips and use them to make new strips, strips where each panel is drawn by a different artist, like a kind of inky relay, and then assembled into some kind of narrative. As pointless and gratuitous as all this may sound, the results are often surprisingly moving, eerie and poetic. And funny.

The constraints employed by Ou-Ba-Po can be divided roughly into two groups. Generative constraints offer tools with which to create new works, while Transformative constraints modify an existing work.

'As pointless and gratuitous as all this may sound, the results are often surprisingly moving, eerie and poetic. And funny.'

Right
Vacances de l'Oubapo
By Jochen Gerner

Opposite page
TNT en Amérique
2002
By Jochen Gerner.
Published by L'Ampoule

'I'm on the borders of several domains. This can be pleasant, but quite confusing too. In this way, I don't feel part of the world of classical comics'

Generative constraints can consist of limiting the reader's point of view, reversibility, palindromes, repetition of one image or graphic element, random sequences etc. Restrictions feature heavily.

Transformative constraints can most easily be applied to already existing comic strips. This technique was used in Situationist texts in the sixties. Slogans were inserted into the word balloons of random comic strips taken from newspapers or advertisements. Another Transformative constraint (again borrowed from OuLiPo) is the enigmatic N+7 method in which each noun is substituted by the seventh noun of a dictionary. How this can be applied to comics, which are by nature pictorial, is anybody's guess.

L'Association (and Ou-Ba-Po) co-founder Killoffer tried his luck. He then proposed an even more esoteric constraint: the Double Blind. This truly long-winded idea takes a comic strip containing both drawings and text. The two are separated and one artist creates new text for the now wordless strip while another draws a new strip for the imageless text. The new text and new drawings are then combined to make yet another new strip, a million miles from the original. Whew.

Another transformative piece is Jochen Gerner's *TNT en Amérique* (L'Ampoule, 2002.) Gerner takes Hergé's *Tintin in America* and proceeds to black-out every page of the original book, leaving only isolated words and floating objects: guns, shoes, cars, etc. (which he then re-drew) all suspended in space. What Gerner has created here is a minimalist graphic novel with no characters and no story. All neon, night time and noise, *TNT* is a book about violence and money and speed and religion. And cities. And America. And Tintin.

Steven: You do so much work. You're a cartoonist, designer, an illustrator, you've written and illustrated children's books. How would you describe yourself and what you do? Jochen Gerner: I was not really a fan of comic art when I was younger. I read comic strips from time to time. But I was very interested in drawing in all its forms. I used to draw a lot, but not with the idea of sequential narration in mind. I rather used to multiply the details in my drawings to develop different degrees of readings. I was attracted by images and literature. I experimented [with] different kinds of narrations and graphic constructions in the laboratory review of l'Association, *Lapin*.

It was when I joined the Ou-Ba-Po in 1998 that I really discovered the unlimited investigation field of comic art. I have always created comics at the same time as other works. Now I am continually trying to make different things, experiment with narrative systems and use new graphic techniques. I collaborate with artists and graphic designers on specific books. I'm on the borders of several domains. This can be very pleasant, but quite confusing too. In this way, I don't feel part of the world of classical comics which try to produce commercial collections and fiction series with a recurrent hero. My aim is not to flatter the readers. My books are generally well received by cultural or artistic magazines, but I've got the impression that some critics specialized in comics are sometimes disconcerted by the most experimental of

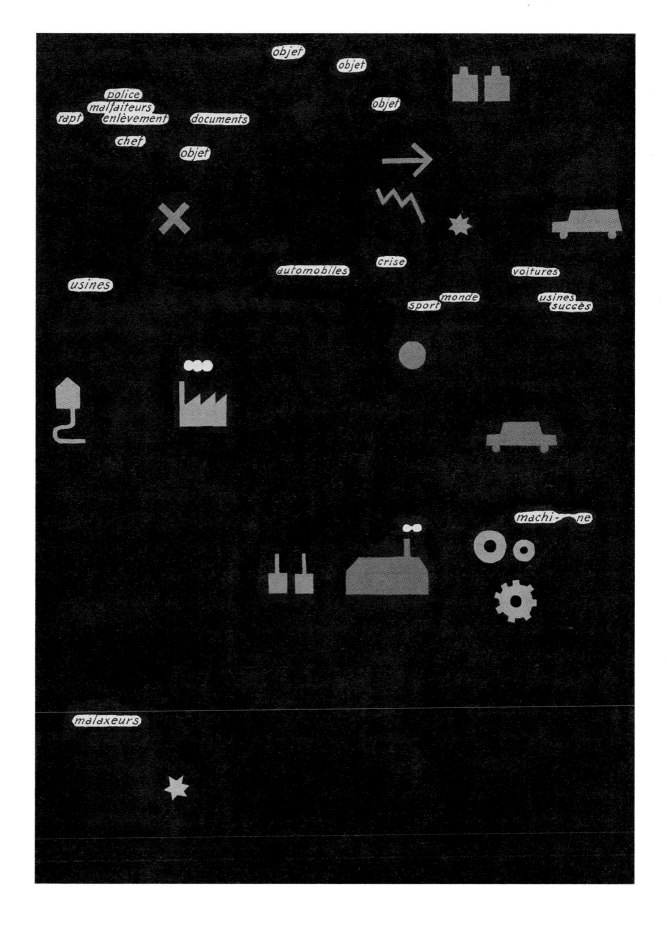

my books (misappropriation of comics, deconstruction of narrative processes). I disturb the narrative codes and the usual systems of representation (square and balloons) that are sacred and irremovable elements for many specialists of comics.

Steven: How do you define Ou-Ba-Po? Jochen: I define Ou-Ba-Po as the most exciting laboratory of experimentations for comic art and for the relationship between text and images. **Steven: Can you explain how you came to do TNT en Amérique?** Jochen: The project was born in the context of Ou-Ba-Po reflections, exercises and experiences. I tried to find new levels of reading. I tried to decode what existed and to discover what didn't exist. I de-structured the raw material to reconstruct it differently, in another way.

I worked for some time on the analysis of the comic book *Tintin in America* by Hergé and particularly on the phenomenon of the fall of bodies that is recurrent in the book. I wanted to do something with it. I began to focus my attention more particularly on the theme of violence. The style of the *ligne claire* (clear line) always tends to soften the violence and to make it banal. A punch in reality is far more violent than what we can see in this kind of book, and I decided that it could be a good occasion to realize an Ou-Ba-Po exercise across a whole book.

I began to analyse and dissect the text in the balloons written by Hergé in *Tintin in America*. Then I choose some words for their meaning (links with violence and recurrent themes relating to American society) and for their musicality. I made out several lists. I was trying to create a set of themes. At that time, I began to cover the pages of Hergé with black colour leaving out only the words that seemed important to me. I found a graphic solution, which consisted in enriching the black colour thanks to 'openings' in the colour. In that way, I could complete the text by visual elements. Then the black colour became a kind of night because all the little spots of colours (signs, pictograms, simple symbols) could appear like little urban lights, like flashing pop neon lighting in the violent obscurity of the American city. It was a kind of sprawling town observed at night from the sky or a promontory.

The black colour was a reference to censure, to the night, the obscurity, evil, the mystery of things not entirely revealed. I worked directly on printed editions by cutting the pages one by one and by covering them with a deep coat of black ink until it was impossible to see elements of the original work through the pages.

My publisher wanted me to rewrite myself the selected words because the handwritten text of Hergé can't be reproduced without authorization. My work of misappropriation in *TNT en Amérique* has disconcerted critics of comics magazines because they tried to read it as if it were a comic book, that is to say with a traditional reading schedule, whereas it was not a comic book anymore.

*   *   *

In 2002 L'Association published *676 Apparitions of Killoffer*, arguably the first Ou-Ba-Po graphic novel. It begins in a fairly straight manner. Our man is flying back to Paris from a trip to Montreal. But he knows a sink full of month-old dirty dishes awaits his return. Panels, text, all of that. Published this year in English by Typocrat, the book rapidly descends into a wordless, panel-less sprawl as Killoffer finds himself multiplied again and again. 676 times. Dozens of Killoffers tumble and brawl across the pages while our man (he's the good guy for once) looks on in mute horror before being dragged into the inky orgy of his many sweaty selves. Somehow Killoffer (the artist) is able to keep enough control over the chaos of his creation. It remains readable despite the fact that each and every one of these monstrous creations looks just like him.

Killoffer (the artist) says that, 'It's experimenting with new ways of doing things, and discovering new narrative styles. And yes, the rules and constraints enable all that.'

Sadly, the most severe constraint applied to comics (at least in English-speaking countries) is the conservatism of readers and publishers alike who consistently overlook the most significant and innovative graphic art form of the past century.

*   *   *

Matt Madden's *99 Ways to Tell A Story – Exercises in Style* is published by Jonathan Cape in July
Killoffer's *676 Apparitions of Killoffer* is published by Typocrat
Jochen Gerner's *TNT en Amerique* is published by L'Ampoule
Lewis Trondhiem's *Nimrod* is published by Fantagraphics

www.mattmadden.com
www.exercisesinstyle.com
www.typocrat.com
www.lampoule.com
www.newhatstories.com
(a site for unofficial American Ou-Ba-Po projects)

Opposite
676 Apparitions of Killoffer (detail)
2002
By Killoffer. Originally published in French in 2002 by l'Association, now published in English by Typocrat.

'It's experimenting with new ways of doing things, and discovering new narrative styles. And yes, the rules and constraints enable all that.'

The Life & Times Of Sponge Bob

Maziar Raein

Recently, I have found myself obsessed by the life and times of SpongeBob, which is a strange predicament to be caught in, for a man of my age. During idle moments, I catch myself wondering about this wondrous creature and his adventures! He has been haunting me for the last few months, as I encounter him in the various nooks and crannies of my imagination.

I had never heard of SpongeBob before, and my introduction to him was casual, as is the way with these things. I was at a party and a friend of mine called out across the room to Robert, a mutual acquaintance of ours. To my astonishment he shouted, 'Oi! SpongeBob, are you going to hog that bottle all night?' Naturally, I thought the reference was to his 'over indulgence' in drink. I earnestly asked, 'Has he got a drinking problem?'. I was put straight.

By the way, unless you have children or you do the slacker thing of watching cartoons on television, you will not know of SpongeBob. He is a cartoon character, or more precisely a sea sponge (though he looks more like a bath sponge in shorts), that lives in a pineapple at the bottom of the sea with his pet snail Gary.

Ever since this first introduction, various forces in my life have conspired in order to make me aware of SpongeBob. He turns up in the most unusual places. For all I know he may have always existed, but I had never noticed him before and it is this process that intrigues me.

You see, SpongeBob is not my first minor obsession. I have had a long line of these infatuations running all the way back to my childhood. Examples of 'minor obsession' over recent years have included my collections of stories about the eccentricity of the Japanese; school exercise books; second hand glasses; ironic English phrases; humour drawn from letters to the editor of *Viz* magazine; observations about the history of men's tailoring (e.g., what is

the difference between English and French vents on a jacket, and was the actor Guy Rolfe the first man to introduce French vents to England? How obscure is that?); the Kabbalistic system and Abjad magic squares; etc. The list goes on, and I know the pattern and the characteristics of my behaviour. For a period, my interest will focus around a subject and, as if by magic, I will constantly tumble across facts, figures, places, people and stories that relate to the subject. In time, my attention will move on, but I will keep that particular folder open, as a kind of work in progress. However, the focus of my attention will shift to something else.

How attention works is unclear to me, and at times in my life, I have desperately struggled to exert control over my capacity to pay attention to things. At school I was unable to focus on almost anything (especially if the fourth year girls' netball team was practicing outside my geography class) and my inability to remember facts and figures was desperately frustrating. There were rare occasions when my attention did function admirably and I was able to focus on a subject. That was when someone told me a story. In fact, it would be safe to say that stories saved me from going mad, since they allowed me to pay attention to the ideas that were encapsulated in them.

The nature of attention is closely aligned to the way we live our lives. For me, life has become no more than a series of stories. They describe the landscape of my attentions. They evolve, intertwine, and create the person that is me.

'There was one who wasn't...'

I was lucky enough to grow up in the Middle East, where the oral culture still dominates, and I was exposed to numerous stories. I repeatedly harangued my parents, family and even strangers to tell me their stories, and if they were too busy, then there were books. All the stories of my childhood began with the charismatic opening phrase *Yeki bood ke nabbod,* or 'There was one who wasn't'. These stories ranged from the Brothers Grimm to Sinbad's adventures in the *Thousand and One Nights*, and interspersed amongst them were the endless jokes that we told about Mullah Nasrudin's latest adventures. The Mullah Nasrudin is a trickster figure that appears in Middle Eastern lore, and the corpus of stories about him is immense. Every taxi driver and teashop owner will spin you a tale of Mullah Nasrudin. In these stories, he behaves in an eternally wise manner and yet at the same time he is foolish. Or rather, he appears to be foolish in order to make a point, about the absurdity of our behaviour as human beings.

For me there are many different types of stories: the traditional stories of my childhood, fables and fairy tales, teaching stories, family stories